THE
CREATIVE
NUDGE

Simple Steps to Help You
THINK
DIFFERENTLY

Mick Mahoney & Kevin Chesters

Laurence King Publishing

'Creativity makes life more fun and more interesting.'

Edward de Bono

CONTENTS

If You
Know What
You're Doing,
STOP
D**O**I**N**G it

DON'T
BELIEVE
WHAT
YOU'RE
TOLD

Don't
Be
Afraid
to Be
Afraid

Let
Chaos
IN

Don't Settle

Be
un-
rea-
son-
able

Hate Consensus

DON'T
RUSH
IT

Failure
Is an
Option

You can't teach people how to be creative

That's because we are all born creative, with the ability to think laterally. To problem-solve creatively in everyday life. Capable of original ideas and thoughts. So, the good news is that it's already in there. It hasn't gone for good or shrunk, no matter how long it has been since you last saw it. Your creative self is sitting there patiently, waiting for you.

Creativity isn't a job title. It's not about being an artist. Creativity isn't even about being able to draw (despite what your art teacher may have told you). Some of the least creative people we know can draw brilliantly. Creativity is a way of looking at the world in whatever field you are in. Even a big muddy field. There's creativity in every industry, every walk of life. Breakthroughs in science or technology don't come by accepting what people have already told us. The future is in the hands of creative thinkers.

Creativity demands that you force your brain out of autopilot. Engage it. Train it to accept new things. Creativity is being brave enough to do new things in new ways – exhilarated by the challenge and the fear. It's about taking risks. Being open to new ideas. Following your own path. Turning your back on the familiar and the ordinary. It's about being extraordinary. Creativity unlocks the door to a more colourful and vibrant world of possibilities. Yes, of course it's a bit scary. But where would the fun be if it wasn't?

Imagine being able to look and think beyond the constraints and pressures life imposes on you. Imagine being able to sprinkle a little magic onto the mundane. It only takes a few simple nudges.

It doesn't matter who you are, how old you are or what you do for a living, you were born with the ability to think creatively. It's time to unleash it.

You can only teach people how not to be creative.

Creativity is something that we unlearn. Evolution, society, education, the workplace, life, all do a great job in helping us to unlearn it. They tell us how to think, how to behave, how to fit in. Don't rock the boat, stick to what you know, failure's not an option. These insidious little thought worms are holding you back. It's very unlikely that there was a point in your life when you decided that you were no longer going to be in any way creative. Instead, creativity has been stolen from you bit by tiny bit without you even noticing. As creatures we are desperate to fit in – to be accepted by the herd. It's how we have learned to survive. We're hard-wired to emulate the behaviours of others. This is the reason why the fashion industry, for one, is so successful; we signal our desire to identify with others. Why else would rational beings all wear ripped jeans, then flares, then skinny fit, then stone wash, then hipsters? To reverse the process, we're going to help you overcome this *biological* and *sociological* double whammy and let all that wonderful, brave, original creative thinking come flooding back into your life.

So, all you need to do is unlearn everything.

Don't worry. It's easier than it sounds. Well, we say it's easy more to encourage you than because we really believe it. Nothing worth doing is ever easy. But it is possible.

Here's how

The brain's connections are like a series of roads. The things you know are built like highways, and the things you don't, like single-lane mud tracks. The more familiar you are with a thought or a concept, i.e. the more it is drummed into you, the stronger the connection will be. This means our brains default to working with what we know. So, basically, unless you have an intense and passionate curiosity that forces you to challenge it, your brain's sat nav will always default to taking you to the main road. This book aims to give you the tools to turn off that main road, start to embrace the mud track, and reclaim your creativity. Those tools are nudges.

Wait – what is a 'nudge'?

Before we get going on our journey to unleash your creative you, a quick note on nudges. Chances are you haven't heard of them yet. Don't worry, by the time you've got to the end of this book, not only will you be bristling with creativity, you'll also be something of an expert on the humble but powerful nudge.

What is a nudge? At its most basic a nudge is a little change to our behaviour or thought patterns that can have a disproportionately large impact on an outcome. A nudge can be making things a little easier, a little simpler and sometimes, a little more motivating. Leaving your gym kit next to your bed so you're more likely to go to the gym in the morning – that's a nudge. The closely spaced aisles in supermarkets that make us feel like we're travelling too fast, so we slow down and buy the items they want us to buy. That's a nudge too. Putting pictures of kids on road signs to get us to slow down. All simple nudges that can have a huge effect.

Nudges can often seem obvious but as humans we become such creatures of habit that we frequently need to be prodded, both metaphorically and physically, into waking up to the possibilities of the world around us. Nudges can be as simple as renaming or reframing things so that we think of them in a different, and more positive, way. Like the brilliant Organising Committee for the London 2012 Olympic Games, renaming 'volunteers' as 'Games Makers'. It entirely changed the way we viewed a worthy chore. Who on earth wouldn't want to be an Olympic Games Maker? It became the hottest ticket of the entire Games. Another simple nudge of this kind was renaming the non-drinker on a night out as the 'Designated Driver' – instantly transforming a zero into a hero.

A nudge is the choice, the action, the use of language or 'the thing' that nudges us in a particular direction – influencing how we see the world and decide to act. Nudges don't require a big lifestyle change. You don't have to become a monastic devotee or find an extra three hours in your day for a difficult set of rules and regulations. No one has the time for that. The key to nudges is that they are small, simple changes that can have surprisingly far-reaching effects. (Probably why they are called 'nudges' and not 'shoves'.)

'Nudge theory' has been about for a while, but in scientific terms it is barely out of nappies. It is part of a field of study called behavioural economics that won a Nobel Prize in 2002. It was such a new thing that the Nobel laureate in question, Daniel Kahneman, had effectively invented a whole new science. In 2010, the UK government, realizing the potential power of nudges to shape the behaviours of the population, launched the world's first 'nudge unit'. It proved so successful that there are now hundreds across the globe, including the highly influential Social and Behavioral Sciences Team in the USA and the Behavioural Insights Unit in New South Wales, Australia. These small, often invisible, interventions have had us doing all sorts of things that we don't really want to do but, in truth, are mostly for our own good. Like paying our taxes on time, driving at a safe speed, even cutting down on sugar. Let's face it, if they were things that we really wanted to do, chances are we would probably be doing them already.

As knowledge of nudge theory spreads, we are being nudged more and more. Unfortunately, though, not always in the right direction. From elections to referendums to radicalization, it is all too easy for people with bad intentions to take something that should be good and use it for ill. Now no longer the preserve of governments and academia, nudges are being heavily invested in by big business, eager to get you to buy this thing over that thing, or take this path over that one, while convincing you that it was your idea all along.

But we want to focus on the use of nudges for a positive outcome. We want to use these little actions to make you – yes, YOU – a more creative person. Nudges have been widely discussed and implemented in the political corridors and boardrooms of the world. Now we want to bring them into living rooms, so that we can all use them to help realize our hopes and dreams, and benefit from being a little more aware of when others are nudging us. Nudge theory is too interesting, too big and too important to leave in the hands of a chosen few; we want to set it free in the wider world. We want to put the power of nudges into your hands. To help you unleash that amazing person that's inside you – your inner creative genius. Go easy though. They're a lot more powerful than they look.

How to use this book

The titles of each of the nine chapters of this book are the nine behaviours that you will embrace to rediscover your creativity. Each chapter explains the sociological and biological reasons why those behaviours are currently inhibited in you. We then explain what you need to do to force your way through those barriers, and we give you the nudges that enable you to succeed.

Each chapter offers a handful of nudges. You only need to build one of them into your day for things to start to change. The important thing is to choose the nudge you feel most able to do. Obviously, the more nudges you embrace over time, the better.

After all your efforts to embed these nudges into the fabric of your life, how will you be able to prove that you are more creative than when you started? Well, we're glad you asked.

Allow us to introduce you to the Remote Associates Test, or RAT for short. This simple method can scientifically track how creative you are. Devised by the much-lauded US psychiatrist Sarnoff A. Mednick and his wife Martha T. Mednick, it was first published in 1959 and refined over the next decade. It remains one of the most standard, and certainly simplest, ways of testing your powers of creative thinking. You'll be given a set of three apparently unrelated words – the challenge is to work out what fourth word might link them. It may be a simple methodology, but that doesn't mean that it is easy.

Here's an example:

Rocking,

Wheel,

High.

The linking word is 'Chair'.

That's a very easy example, just in case you're feeling smug.

Here's a slightly harder example:

Luck, Belly, Honey.

The linking word is 'Pot'.

Actually, that was still pretty easy. Sorry.

At the end of each chapter we'll give you two RATs to do. Over the course of the book, and as you get to grips with the nudges, they should become easier to solve.

If You
Know What
You're Doing,
STOP
D**O**/NG it

It's comforting to place yourself in familiar surroundings, think familiar thoughts and do familiar things. You often hear the phrase, 'I know what I like, and I like what I know'. And in such a fast-moving and changing world, it's understandable to feel this way; you are constantly under threat from change and it can be tough to keep facing into it. But when it comes to creativity, avoiding change is a cardinal sin. It's the worst of the worst. It's Chapter 1 in the book of how *not* to be creative. Fight that urge to stay within your comfort zone with everything you have. It's an ever-decreasing creative circle. It stunts your creative faculties. It makes you resistant to new thoughts and ideas. It holds you back, like a pernicious and clingy boy/girlfriend who doesn't want you to change because they are worried that you'll outgrow them and leave them behind in their familiar little world.

The very essence of creativity is to embrace the new. New ideas. New concepts. New people. New ways of approaching familiar things. Open your eyes and your mind to new possibilities. Try it. No, really. Try it. Pursue new for all you are worth. Sticking with what you know is never going to lead to a new outcome or fresh thinking. You aren't going to surprise yourself or anyone else. So, it's time to stop. It's not going to be easy. But it will be worth your while.

The science bit

A funny thing happens when we stick to what we know. While we might become faster and more efficient, we actually get lazy. Dangerously lazy. In fact, a third of all car accidents happen within a mile of home – the area that we know best. When we're most comfortable, our brains think that they can switch off, so they do, turning us instantly into creative wet blankets. Familiar territory is dangerous territory.

Try counting the **F's** in this sentence:

Finished files are the result of years of scientific study combined with the experience of years.

3? 4? NO. 6!
Finished files are the result of years of scientific study combined with the experience of years.

Well done if you got them all. But chances are you didn't. That's because we're all so familiar and comfortable with reading that we often miss words like 'of'. So, what else have you been missing?

The science behind this is known as '**inattentional blindness**', or '**perceptual blindness**'. It's nothing to do with your eyes and everything to do with your brain. Our attention is only ever directed at a small number of things, and we miss the rest. Inattentional blindness is a psychological lack of attention. Simply put, we don't see what we *don't expect* to see.

So why do we stick to what we know? Nature can explain. Our brains love conserving energy. It takes a lot of juice to run a brain (enough to run a light bulb, in fact), so we have evolved to default to 'low power mode' when we can. This effect is called '**habituation**', and the brain uses it to drown out the ordinary and expected in order to prioritize new stimuli coming in. We have essentially evolved to turn off our unnecessary notifications. If we've heard it, seen it, felt it or smelt it before, it'll be edited out. Think about when you first sit down on a chair in a coffee shop. Let's say it's soft but keeps its shape. In the beginning your brain registers that feeling ... but it soon stops doing that because you no longer need an update – you now need to focus on something else. The same is true for the effectiveness of many drugs; they become less effective with repeated use.

For those of you who have moved house to a busy road, you'll notice that the sound of traffic outside disappears from your attention after only a few weeks. We don't consciously process things that happen repetitively and predictably because we don't need to. We have evolved an auto-mode that takes hints from what we expect to happen rather than having to process everything fresh, and we can operate largely on expectations over reality. If we had to consciously process all of the world all of the time, life would be exhausting.

This is a black-and-white photo. Look again. See it now? Your brain expects to see colours thanks to the hints from the lines superimposed on the photo, and so you see them. We see a lot more with our brains than we do with our eyes. So, we'll say it again, if you think you know what you're doing, stop doing it.

However, this auto-mode is not helpful when we're thinking about being creative. We don't want to recycle old thoughts from well-trodden paths. We want to form new ideas. Now, people naturally gravitate to and like what is familiar – if we've been exposed to it in the past and it hasn't killed us, then that's a good thing. This is true almost everywhere. The colour in our bathroom grows on us over time, we begin to love that ugly chair or child, and the more familiar our environment becomes, the more our brain feels comfortable with switching into automatic. We're programmed to save power, but creative thinking is not a low-power task.

Our society and environment can also hold us back creatively; the world is designed with our auto-mode in mind. Modern technology perpetuates the familiar. Our GPS systems and public transport apps help us set consistent routes home; we create consistent 'morning playlists' and programme our coffee machines to kick into gear at 7:05. In standardizing and micro-managing our experience of the world, we risk also creating an environment that's less stimulating or challenging, yet more often than not, creativity lies in friction. So, how might we break the shackles of comfort and familiarity to engage our brain and benefit from a little more friction?

THE ANTIDOTE:
Do familiar things in unfamiliar ways

Are you starting to see just how damaging familiarity is to creativity? In fact, it's pretty dangerous all round. Now, don't get us wrong – we like a little familiarity as much as the next person. A cup of tea. A pair of old Blundstone boots. A roast on a rainy Sunday. But all in moderation. So, what's it going to be, comfy cosy or scary new? Are you ready to unleash your creative beast, or at least let him poke his beautiful head out into the sunlight for the first time in a very long while? Yes. Of course you are. You've got this.

We've created a bunch of nudges that are specifically designed to stop you and your brain from defaulting automatically to what you know. Simple, familiar actions done differently that will shunt your brain off the tarmac and onto the off-road tracks. These nudges will make you crave the new. Open your mind to new stimuli and challenges, and over time encourage yourself to run a mile from the unoriginal. You only need to incorporate one of them into your day for things to trigger change. Start with the one that you think you'll find easiest. Then, when you're ready, add a second.

1.

Apples and pears

Go and get yourself an apple – or a pear, if you prefer. You're now going to demonstrate just how easy it is to snap out of 'sticking with what you know', and make yourself instantly more creative. Pick up your apple. Hold it in your non-dominant hand. (That's the one you don't use much.) Take a bite.

You are now more creative and open to new ways of thinking than you were only moments earlier: amazing but true. Simply by overriding habits in one area you will disrupt the familiar and challenge the brain to respond and adapt, keeping its neural pathways buzzing. Studies show that by deliberately opening doors with your non-dominant hand, or stirring your tea in the opposite direction, you can actually increase your self-control and consequently your ability to stop your brain from nodding off. Meaning, such alterations can inspire you to embrace the new. So, why not try putting stickers on everyday items – fruit, mugs, handles – to remind yourself?

This is what makes nudges so brilliant and successful. They really can be this simple when you know what you're doing. Don't mistake their apparent simplicity for lack of power. They are powerful *because* they are so simple.

2.

A better rule of thumb

A tech take on this is to change your smartphone log-in to your non-dominant thumb. And if you're feeling particularly punchy you could try texting or dialling with your non-dominant hand, too. But don't overdo it. It's far better that you build nudges into your everyday life rather than binge on them and then forget all about them.

3.

Walk the other way

Another very simple nudge is to take a different route to work or school. You'll arrive buzzing with a renewed creative energy. They won't recognize you. Start by taking one different road. Then the next day another different road. Then two. Build it up slowly. Then eventually take a different route entirely. Get off at a different tube, tram or bus stop and walk. Yes, it will make you late some days but creativity demands sacrifice. But please don't get lost. Unless of course you want to, in which case, get very lost. That will really get that brain of yours sparking.

4.

Talk to strangers

'I like to meet new people.' A friend of ours lives in a ski resort in the Italian Alps. For several months of the year his remote, delightfully rustic mountain village is besieged by thousands of holidaymakers eager to enjoy the dramatic slopes, family-run restaurants and lively bars. He is a very talented skier, smart and confident, but not one of life's most outgoing and chatty young men. One season he sported a T-shirt that bore the legend 'I like to meet new people'. Ironic or otherwise, it sparked many conversations with complete strangers whom he would otherwise not have spoken to. This was probably the opposite of what he really wanted to happen – nevertheless, it proved to be a very positive and mind-expanding experience. Forcing yourself to talk to strangers, perhaps someone on your bus route or even that person at school or work whom you see every day but never engage with, will force you to hear new points of view, thoughts and ideas.

See how many new conversations you can manage. Aim for at least three a week. More would be great, but quality matters more than quantity. Take your time and properly engage in the conversation. Be prepared to have your own thoughts challenged. For the more confident among you, why not get the T-shirt printed and wear it with a smile?

If you are a little less forward, going to a new place works in a very similar way to having a new conversation but without the attendant social awkwardness. It jolts your brain into action. Unfamiliarity is a neurological double espresso.

Defamiliarize your selfie

Write a list of 10 places that you have never been to. A cricket match. A rodeo. A mosque. A Korean BBQ. A men-only sauna. Grimsby. Paris, Texas. Next door. (These are some of our 10.) Then work your way down your list. Yes, really. And no, you can't change your list. The whole point is to take you out of your comfort zone.

At each place take a selfie. Use that image as your screen-saver. It will remind you of the incredible new experience you had and spur you on to the next one.

Lose your keys, find yourself

The final nudge in this chapter is for the risk takers. We call it the 'Where are my valuables?' nudge. We all tend to keep our valuables (think phone, keys, etc.) in the same place all the time. Maybe it's the bottom of your handbag, maybe it's your front-right pocket. But doing that is living with the familiar, doing what you've always done, so try this. Keep one of your valuables in a new bag or pocket so that you'll have to engage your brain to remember where it is. The spark of fear that is quickly resolved through some conscious thinking could be the mindful moment that stops you living on auto.

And breathe. Whichever nudge, or nudges, you chose, you are now firmly on the road to setting all that wonderful creativity free ... and some of you will have lost your keys.

Sausage, Chilli, Hot.

Cabbage, Work, Eye.

(Answers at the back of the book.)

DON'T BELIEVE WHAT YOU'RE TOLD

Received wisdom is, without question, the worst kind of wisdom to receive. Received wisdom is merely what other people have accepted as being right. It doesn't mean it's always going to be right for you. Or even right at all. Ask a million questions. Trust no one – only your own instincts. Yes, of course it's hard. And exhausting. But how do you think anything new was ever discovered, thought of, or created? Someone somewhere questioned the status quo. They said, hang on a minute. Really? Why? What if? That someone now needs to be you.

Some of the most ridiculous beliefs have become normalized and accepted as fact, thanks to received wisdom. Hands up everyone who believes that you can see the Great Wall of China from space. Utter nonsense. But enough people have said it over the years, so it has become broadly accepted as fact.

Careful! It's dangerous to wake a sleepwalker. In fact, it's more dangerous *not* to wake a sleepwalker. Statistically, they are far more likely to hurt themselves if they are left alone.

Baby birds. Remember when you were a kid and you found a baby bird that had fallen out of the nest? You called it Jeff, and you wanted to take it home and look after it, but everyone told you not to pick it up because its parents would no longer recognize its smell if you did? Birds have next to no sense of smell. Yes, really.

The science bit

The truth is often merely what everyone is prepared to accept as the truth. It doesn't mean it is the truth. And it's not always easy to get to the truth. In fact, research tells us that we're lied to between 10 to 200 times a day. We promise ;). This is particularly scary when you consider that we've actually evolved to determine what the 'facts' are through conversation and agreement within social groups – 'It's true because they said it was true!' If you think of Wikipedia and Reddit, not a great deal has changed.

Unfortunately, however, rather than striving to establish and share the true facts, the prospect of being able to convince others, and benefit ourselves, has meant that most of our evolutionary smarts have been dedicated to manoeuvring our social position rather than telling the truth.

If we can convince people of a truth that's favourable to us, if we can twist the facts in our direction, then we can have control. We're status seekers, not always truth seekers. Surely not. Not that nice Mrs Jones. Not your best friend, Bjorn. Not Dr Singh. Father Mulrooney. Yep. Afraid so. And before you get on your moral high horse, you're guilty too. You tell a couple of juicy fat ones a day, just like everyone else. So, in this tricky world where honesty comes second, we rely on other factors to help determine what we should and shouldn't believe. This isn't a calculation of the facts at play, it's a simple question: 'Do I trust the person telling me?'

Research tells us that *who* delivers the information or facts is often more powerful than the information itself. This is known as the '**messenger effect**'. If we see that person to be similar to us, someone who looks credible or authoritative, we instinctively trust and obey them. However, this can be easily abused. Stanley Milgram's now infamous obedience studies in the 1960s showed that an experimenter, who was really an actor, could encourage complete strangers to administer a potentially fatal voltage of electricity to an unsuspecting participant simply by wearing a 'credible' white jacket and telling them the experiment must continue. In another study, when encouraged to gift a coin to help a stranger's expired parking meter, compliance levels soared from 45 per cent when the stranger was dressed as a blue collar worker, to 82 per cent when asked by someone dressed in a firefighter's uniform.

The impact of more subtle **cues of authority** can be equally powerful – in fact, one experiment found 350 per cent more people were willing to follow a man crossing the street against a red light and against the traffic when he wore a suit rather than casual clothes. This is the basic premise behind the brand spokesman in advertising. It's why brands will pay fortunes to people they know you are willing to follow or believe in. YouTubers. Instagram influencers. Actors. Sporting heroes.

The lesson here is to be careful of cues of authority, and even our propensity to believe people we like. Just because they look the part, hold high status or are wearing a shiny badge, doesn't mean they're always right – or even that they have your best interests at heart. All it really means is that they might be being paid enough to cross their integrity thresholds.

In addition to *who* tells us, the way in which information is relayed can be just as influential in helping lies 'stick'. Psychological studies show that the more visual, visceral and concrete the information, the more 'mentally available' the information becomes, and the more likely we are to recall, retain and believe it. It's why we're more likely to follow dietary advice when we visualize a meal as the equivalent number of burgers or doughnuts rather than just talk about calories, and why a jury is more likely to believe that a car was speeding if it was reported to 'smash' into another, as opposed to merely 'bump' it. It's no wonder we all believe the Great Wall of China can be seen from space. The lesson? If you can draw it or picture it mentally, you're more likely to believe it.

Modern media has learned that the 'visual' and 'concrete' captures our attention and sways us. Social media algorithms push out sensationalized materials because they are known to generate a response. Fake news is the new reality for many. It's becoming close to impossible to know the difference between real and fake any more, so it has never been more important to question everything.

We are surrounded by 'appointed authority' and over-inflated titles. Chiefs, Directors, Presidents and Principals. As soon as we're out of nappies we're positioned as an authority in something, irrespective of ability. The problem with this is that once the authority is there, be it Library Monitor or Police Officer, we're blinded by it and follow wholeheartedly. Our daily language does us no favours either. Aphorisms seep into our consciousness, repeated by our nearest and dearest; they're on every mug, every kitchen wall and everyone's lips, ready to go and reinforce the gospel of received wisdom bullshit. Psychologists call this phenomenon the '**mere-exposure effect**' and it means that we're more trusting of things we see more frequently and are more familiar with. If you see 12 times a day that 'with hope anything is possible' then the chances are you might stop relying on things like hard work and perseverance.

THE ANTIDOTE: Question everything

Everything. Push past the stuff that everyone else accepts.

Look at the vintage cigarette ad below featuring a doctor promoting smoking. It seems ridiculous now, but what is its modern equivalent? Question every orthodoxy. Every status quo. Every fact. Every pernicious piece of received wisdom. Ask, 'Why?' Think, 'What if?' You'll get to somewhere different and interesting. You'll spark a new thought. A different way to come at something.

Yes, you will drive people around you nuts. But creativity is the pursuit of the truth – and of new truths. Creativity doesn't accept. It questions, it agitates. Now, obviously you can't just decide that from today on you'll refuse to listen to anyone or believe in anything. That way lies serious medication. And our aim isn't to turn you into a raging argumentalist.

In truth, the object here is to get you to think for yourself, to feel comfortable holding an original point of view. And with a carefully applied nudge you will be on the road. Remember, it's better to pick the nudge that can become a part of your everyday life than to binge on them all for a few days then get overwhelmed and give up. You've already waited this long to rediscover that creative spark.

It's question time

Get two different-coloured marker pens. Every time you hear or see some steaming lump of received wisdom or fanatical fact, write it on a piece of paper in one colour. For example: 'You can see the Great Wall of China from space.' Then with the other marker turn it into a question. 'Can you see the Great Wall of China from space?' Immediately you're forced to think. Weigh up the likelihood. Look into it. Have a point of view. Not just accept. Challenging everything can be hard, given our extreme readiness to obey authority. It's going to take a bit of practice before it's second nature.

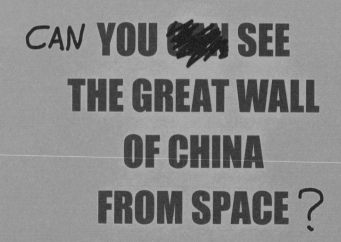

2.

Keep scrolling on

Very sensibly, our brains are designed to conserve energy for when we really need it. As previously mentioned, they default to the easy path. This makes them disinclined to ask questions and seek answers after a plausible answer has been presented.

From now on, you're not going to be fobbed off by the first page of Google, or whichever search engine you use to seek answers. Push on – see what else pops up when you start to dig into the murky depths of page 4, or even 5, if you're feeling particularly adventurous. Look into some of the other explanations. Especially the more far-fetched ones. You could even get really crazy and go to the library for a little old-school book research. Who knows what kind of journey you'll end up taking?

3.

Get Sherlock on it

This little nudge could not be simpler. Find something Sherlockian that reminds you to question everything. For example, a mini magnifying glass, a deerstalker, a mini Sherlock vinyl. Place it somewhere prominent – on a key ring, perhaps. He wouldn't accept the first answer. Be more Sherlock.

4.

Swap the hierarchy

You'll need to find some digital visual stimuli for this one – images of people that you really respect and trust. Let's say you've chosen Angelina Jolie and Sheryl Sandberg, for argument's sake.

Or it could be David Beckham, Gandhi or a heroic firefighter. Now swap out the photos in your phone contacts. No need to go crazy and change everyone's; just go for a couple of your work colleagues, a couple of close friends and a couple of family members. Then every time one of them calls you'll get a visual prompt to imagine their voice coming out of the mouth of someone you're predisposed to trust.

Will it change how you view what's being said? It will. At the very least it will show you how hard it is to interpret a message purely on its merits. Challenge yourself to listen to *what* is being said. Not how it's being said. Or by whom.

You don't really believe that, do you?

With a few of the nudges in this book there's a full-blooded, totally committed, up-to-your-neck nudge and then there's a safer, dip-your-toe-in-and-see-how-it-goes version. Next up is one such nudge. We make no judgement about which one you go with. Honestly we don't. Well, maybe a little bit.

From time to time you'll find yourself thinking, 'Does everyone in the room believe this?' Scary, isn't it, when everyone seems to be cultishly accepting of something? You're looking around to see if there are any other sceptical faces. But there aren't.

Groups do very odd things. **Confirmation bias**, which is when people with similar beliefs seek and receive validation from each other, creates the illusion of invulnerability in those beliefs. It results in the death of progress. It closes those minds to new and progressive ideas. The philosopher Bertrand Russell once said, 'The whole problem with the world is that fools and fanatics are always so certain of themselves, and wiser people so full of doubts.'

So, be the one that creates doubt. The next time you find yourself at a meeting or a dinner party or wherever everyone is in violent agreement with each other, take a deep breath and argue the opposite point of view. Be aware that this could get awkward. If their arguments have several sources, and are reasoned and balanced, then chances are there is something in them. Great, you've learned something. If they get worked up at you daring to challenge their fragile dogma, then you were right to call them out on it. Choose where you do something like this carefully, though. Seriously, it's amazing how riled up people can get when you challenge their beliefs. We'll talk about group dynamics in more depth in Chapter 7.

The gentler version of this shifts the emphasis to challenging your beliefs rather than those of others. Much safer, but possibly no less uncomfortable. Questioning everything also means being prepared to question yourself. If you are naturally left leaning politically, look right. And vice versa. Google the opposite point of view to your own.

Every time there is a news item or editorial that piques your interest, read about it from an outlet that has the opposite political or ideological point of view to yours. It may just infuriate you or entrench your existing point of view, but it will open up your mind to another way of looking at things. It really doesn't matter whether you agree with that way. All that matters is that you learn to accept that there are different ways to look at the same thing. And hopefully start to call yourself out.

6.

Time to rhyme

Finally, we're going to end this chapter with a rhyme. We all love a rhyme. Although, rhymes can be surprisingly dangerous in the wrong hands, due to our increased willingness to believe anything if it's said that way – it's known as the **'Keats effect'**. It's why so many successful advertising end-lines do it. You've been warned. Rhymes can also be used to positive effect, though. They're why you remember so many useful hints and tips: 'A stitch in time saves nine', and so on. Well, here's one to help you remember to question everything.

'Don't always be sold on the first thing you're told.'
Repeat that to yourself a few times until it sticks.

Socket, Lid, Brow.

Crystal, Foot, Snow.

(Answers at the back of the book.)

Don't Be Afraid to Be Afraid

Franklin D. Roosevelt famously declared in his presidential inaugural address of 1933, 'The only thing we have to fear is fear itself.' He was talking about the United States in the context of the Great Depression but he could just as easily have been talking about releasing our inner creative genius when he completed the sentence with '... nameless, unreasoning, unjustified terror which paralyses needed efforts to convert retreat into advance.'

If we no longer fear fear, we are free to try new things and see how far embracing change will take us. Let's advance to a more creative outcome. A lot of what it is to be creative is to come to terms with fear and uncertainty.

One of our creative mantras is 'Hate Six'. Let us explain. Think of all creative output on a scale of one to ten. A six is, broadly speaking, OK. In fact, it's better than OK, because it's better than a five; a five is OK. No one gets fired for a six, but no one takes a risk for a six either. A six is the evil child of fear and cowardice. It's safe and comfortable, and it has no place in our creative endeavours. Learn to hate it. True creativity is the pursuit of a nine or a ten, while being aware that despite all your best efforts it can sometimes end up in the hinterlands of a one or a two ... and being OK with that. As creativity expert Sir Ken Robinson might say, we stigmatize failure in schools and in business. We become afraid of it.

This chapter isn't about being comfortable with failure, though – that's Chapter 9. First you need to learn not to be afraid of the fear itself and pursue a creative ten. Letting fear and uncertainty into your life will probably be one of the hardest things you will do in your pursuit of creativity. It removes your stabilizers and forces you to feel uncomfortable. Remember that feeling you had when your mum or dad took the stabilizers off your bike? Terror. Utter terror. Exciting though, wasn't it? OK, so you might have fallen off a few times, cut your knee, cried a bit, sprained your wrist, cried a bit more, run off screaming, kicked your bike, swore you'd never ride again. But every time you tried again, the fear lessened until eventually it went away altogether and was replaced by an incredible sense of freedom.

Don't worry though, we're here to hold onto the saddle, just in case.

The science bit

It's not your fault. We're hard-wired as a species to be negative. We just can't help but assume that the worst is going to happen. Of the six core human emotions (happiness, sadness, surprise, fear, anger, disgust), only one is positive. This shows that we have evolved to deal primarily with a world of negativity. Hardly surprising when you consider the human journey over the last 250,000 years, which has mostly involved trying not to be killed in one way or another.

Fear is the emotional response to our bodies 'gearing up' to address perceived threat. When you feel afraid, your sympathetic nervous system takes over. That's your fight or flight response. Your heart rate increases, your gut switches off (digesting your lunch is less of a priority when faced with a tiger), you begin to sweat and your eyes dilate so you can take in more information, even in darkness. Every last bit of you is

Happiness

Sadness

Surprise

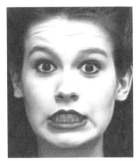

Fear

Anger

Disgust

preparing to fight or run for your life. But, on occasion, you freeze. Game over.

Unpleasant but true: some evolutionary scientists believe that we evolved to sweat heavily in fearful situations so that we would become slippery enough to escape predators. Next time you're standing there dripping and wondering what to say for yourself, you will know why.

It makes evolutionary sense to assume that something will kill you, rather than to wait and see. We're threat detectors, and we experience and remember the world like that. If, for example, you were reviewing a crime scene where a gun was present, you would spend much more of your time following the weapon, to the point where you would find it hard to recall the rest of the picture accurately. We become blind to surrounding information because we've evolved to focus on the threat.

Incredibly, this effect also occurs when a new creative idea makes us feel uncertain about things that we were previously sure of. We can find it genuinely alarming. You only have to see how regularly modern art is met with outraged headlines.

The biochemical changes in our brain make us aggressive, literally fighting the new idea, or make us timid, fleeing from it. How does the sculpture on the right, by Jake and Dinos Chapman, make you feel? The name for this phobia of new things is '**neophobia**'.

Ever been on holiday and experienced such a stressful journey to get there that all you wanted when you arrived was food you were familiar with? An omelette. Your favourite cheese. A cup of tea. That's likely to be because your levels of arousal were so high that the increased arousal from a new food experience would have pushed you over your limit. The same can also explain our desire to listen to a particular playlist over and over again after a break-up. You already have so much to deal with that the novelty of new music is too much to take in.

We humans get really scared when faced with something new. We hate the unknown. Remember being scared of the dark or the wardrobe monster when you were a child? It is perfectly natural for us to fear the unknown more than the 'known bad', because we are hard-wired to do so. But let's think about it for a moment in the context of everyday life in the early twenty-first century. We presume you're reading this in a fairly safe environment like your living room, a train seat or possibly tucked up in bed.

Imagine the times when you are 'scared' in the context of doing something new, professionally or personally. It is unlikely that the negative outcome will involve a life or death result. It is highly improbable that you will come to any actual physical harm. So, in most cases you are 100 per cent safe, from an evolutionary perspective. Research shows that in the context of a safe environment, being scared can be incredibly positive. Good scary. The body's natural 'fight or flight' mechanism can be hijacked when we feel safe; the natural chemicals that our body releases when it is scared can be put to good use. It can even be pleasurable.

'If we're in a situation where we know we're safe, like a haunted house, scary movie, or rollercoaster, think of it as hijacking the flight response and enjoying it. This is similar to a high arousal state, not sexual, but like when we're happy, laughing, excited, or surprised.'

Margee Kerr, Faculty Lecturer in Sociology, University of Pittsburgh, *Scream: Chilling Adventures in the Science of Fear*

This makes perfect sense. Your mind knows you are safe, so it can convert those scary chemicals into pleasure chemicals. Your brain takes you to the edge of danger knowing that it's just make-believe. So, now we know, from an evolutionary perspective, that when you aren't really 'scared' there are incredibly positive benefits to leaving fear behind. In fact, we can accept being scared as a good place to be.

THE ANTIDOTE: Feel-good fear

Good to know that evolution has built you to survive, isn't it? To start to allow fear to play a truly positive role in your life you need to find ways to override all those instincts – to reframe fear as excitement.

Thinking about fear in a different way will enable you to act differently and effect a positive outcome. Are you actually scared or are you just excited in an anticipatory way? Next time you feel nervous, try to appreciate that this is a great thing. This is your body getting ready to fire on all cylinders. This is the time. Tell yourself how excited you are, not how scared you are. And don't just tell yourself – tell other people. Get excited. Get really excited. Get ready to rumble. The more fear you are able to expose yourself to, the more comfortable you will become with it. And hopefully, in time, you'll start to enjoy it, perhaps even seek it out.

Now, obviously, if you are experiencing fear because a large tiger is standing in front of you with its stomach grumbling, then don't try and convince yourself that what you are actually feeling is excitement. You aren't. You're experiencing good old, evolutionary, self-preserving fear.

Run. Now.

THE NUDGES

Remember,
your armour and
your sword are...

Get pumped

Start the day with a coffee and some very loud, very fast music.
Before the day unfolds and carries you along at its usual rhythm,
crank up a thumping track. Lose yourself in it. Down your coffee,
then head for the door. They won't know what's hit them.

Research illustrates that loud, fast-paced music increases
our tolerance for risk. This particular research was based on
your increased likelihood to have unprotected sex or smoke a
joint after listening to loud, fast music. But the principle is the
same. Think of it as marching into battle and having your blood
pumped up by the drums.

Why not put together a playlist? Call it 'Scared of Nothing
or No One'. Dip in every time you're having a bit of a wobble.

The boring diet

This next nudge is ridiculously simple, as indeed the best nudges
always are. But it will take a bit of commitment. And yes, it is
counter-intuitive.

Put yourself on The Boring Diet for 24 hours. Cut back
on all that fun and sensory arousal and get bored. As bored as
possible, ideally. Seriously. Unplug the wifi, stick to old playlists,
avoid trendy new recipes, delete the dating app, spend time with
family and old friends. In fact, do everything you can to avoid any
surprises or anything too stimulating. Stop doing new things. If
you can, monitor your heart rate. Keep it under 100 bpm.

We can only cope with a bit of change at once. By denying yourself you'll become so un-aroused that you'll be craving something dangerous and exciting. If you make it through 24 hours, make it 48 next time. Who knows what you might end up doing after that, you crazy, badass rock 'n' roller.

The name game

Another simple nudge is to rename stuff to make it less intimidating. Many of our workspaces are filled with threatening language that simply goes unnoticed. Embedded within our creative spaces, they prevent us from opening up.

We've all had a brain-STORM. Many of us sit in WAR-rooms trying to be creative. No doubt it works for the military, but it just isn't the environment that generates truly original work. So next time you bring people together, think about how you might make it more 'open' and comfortable. Is it an idea experiment? What about a harvest? Do you create a safe space known as the 'room of possibilities' rather than feeling like you're preparing to go into battle? And if you're really brave, try renaming it the 'ideas jacuzzi' – nothing scary happens in a jacuzzi!

It's all good

Ever faced a scary or difficult situation and wondered, 'What's the best that can happen?' Unlikely. But you're going to from now on. This great little nudge really flies in the face of the five negative emotions and subverts our brain's automatic response to seek the worst outcome. This is called **catastrophizing** and it's hard-wired into you. Catastrophizing stops you from doing all kinds of things that might end up being amazing and life changing. But, with our help you are not going to catastrophize any more. You're going to do whatever the opposite of that is called.

Next time you are faced with a situation that terrifies you, ask yourself, 'What is the best that can happen?', then write a list of all the possible positive outcomes. By asking yourself that simple question you are flooding the one positive emotion you possess with all your creative energy and supercharging it.

The incy-wincy nudge

The final nudge in this chapter only really works if you're scared of spiders. Statistics suggest that is 75 per cent of you. Apologies to the remaining 25 per cent. You might have to use that burgeoning imagination to picture another insect or animal that makes you scream hysterically and wee yourself a bit. We're going to get you to try a little **exposure response prevention therapy**. This is all about getting you to increase your tolerance to fear, by engineering small risks in your life.

OK. Close your eyes. Think of a spider. Good job. So on the blank page opposite, draw a picture of that spider. Don't forget to include its long, hairy legs and eight big eyes. Now, next time you see a spider in your house, stay in the same room as that spider for as long as you can. Keep repeating this process until you no longer feel like screaming when you see one. Then pick it up. Yes, you can. Yes, you will. Creativity is about bravery and sacrifice, remember?

Copy, Tom, Bob.

Tight, Works, Mark.

(Answers at the back of the book.)

Let Chaos IN

'One must still have chaos in oneself to be able to give birth to a dancing star.'

Friedrich Nietzsche

Creativity is born of chaos. No amount of logic is ever going to result in anything magical. It will only ever give you the correct answer to a question. Correct answers are great when a correct answer is what you need. Creativity is not the pursuit of correct answers. It's the pursuit of odd, ill-fitting, fractured brilliance that enables a momentary window into an uplifting and undefinable universe that touches us like nothing else can. The song that stirs every emotion, the film that haunts us for weeks, the idea that changes the world, or the scientific advance that makes us question everything.

Quantum leaps don't come about by following a critical path. That's why you can't industrialize creativity. Computers can't create chaos, and they never will. There is no formula for original thought, which frustrates the bejesus out of the money men.

Great creative brains – the ones society has an ugly habit of stigmatizing as the crazies, the rebels and the outsiders – make the kinds of connections that no one else can. They connect the unconnectable. The more chaotic and messy their minds, the more likely these odd connections are to be made. They've allowed their heads to fill up with amazing things, left them in there to play happily, and waited patiently for their beautiful offspring.

Disorder. Not order. Mixing it up, not sorting it out. You have to be willing to let chaos in. Push against what your brain is trying desperately to get you to do – to find a pattern, to impose order. Fight it. Chaos won't enter your life unless you invite it in by creating the conditions for it to thrive.

True, original creativity needs chaos. You need chaos. Society needs chaos.

The science bit

Once again, the evolutionary brain doesn't help us here. The brain is a pattern-seeking machine. It makes no evolutionary sense to appreciate the beauty of randomness because it doesn't help us to survive or thrive as a species. Because of this, we're forever trying to 'crack the code', or find the eternal answer to life, the universe and everything.

If you were to encourage a mouse to press a lever to receive a reward, and on one occasion it got two pellets, then on another occasion it got one, then none, then five, you'd see the mouse continually press the lever to try and establish the pattern. This is known as **'operant conditioning'**, and it's what we spend our lives doing without even realizing it. It takes a conscious effort to challenge it. Because of our need to make sense of the world, we mistakenly see patterns and meanings in things that have no meaning because our brains demand it. We are creatures of habit, beings who need order, and we'll impose it on ourselves even when we don't need to. There's a term for this – **'apophenia'** (a-poh-fee-nia), if you want to impress your friends.

We have always invented stories to make sense of the world. When our ancestors didn't understand why the sun came up in the morning they invented a sun god to explain it. Then a moon god, and a sea god, and so on. It's where most religions and cults started – the need to explain those things that lacked an explanation.

It also goes a long way to explaining most conspiracy theories. We see or hear about something that doesn't seem quite right, like how the moon landing appeared to be lit like a movie, or how 5G masts were spreading Covid-19 in the spring of 2020, and our brain's need for a narrative makes us susceptible to plausible suggestion. It's how we are regularly preyed upon by unscrupulous individuals or organizations who have a vested interest in us believing one thing over another. A great example of this were the 'Pizzagate' conspiracy theories surrounding Hillary Clinton during the 2016 US presidential election. A fringe rumour created to discredit her by extreme alt-right conspiracy theorists was amplified on social media and eventually travelled all the way to mainstream news sites and official channels such as Fox News.

It's beyond our evolutionary brains to accept that there might not be any patterns, that life is just a random bag of bits. It's why we are ridiculously easy to influence and control. We see patterns in even the most random of things. We see Elvis in grilled cheese sandwiches and animals in rock formations. (Don't pretend that you can't see it.) There's actually a scientific term for that too – yes, the cheese sandwich face thing. It's called '**pareidolia**' (pah-ray-doh-lia). It's all because our brains HATE chaos, which takes an incredible amount of mental energy to process. Your brain would much rather you just got in line.

Annoyingly, our brains also love a bit of **confirmatory information processing**. It means that we prefer information that fits what we already think. Of course we do. It's easier. The brain is always looking for ways to take the easy route. Just to add insult to injury, this **confirmation bias** is more likely to occur when we're in neat and tidy environments. Studies prove that it happens less in messy environments.

Simply, our brains are more creative when surrounded by disorder. Researchers at the University of Minnesota found that working in a messy environment made people more creative. In tests, participants came up with just as many new ideas when working in tidy environments or messy ones, but the ideas generated in messy rooms tended to be more interesting or creative. The data also found that people with messy desks are more prone to risk taking, while those at cleaner desks tend to follow strict rules and are less likely to try new things. And of course creativity is about taking risks and doing new things.

So, make a mess and refuse to tidy it up in the name of creativity. You now have science on your side. Tell others that you're actually priming your mind not to be so sticky and stubborn. And far from being lazy, you are actually pushing your brain to work harder. They should be carrying you shoulder high through the streets, not tutting. Creative infidels.

Basically, your brain is a bit of a slob that is diddling you out of your creative birthright. You're not going to let it get away with that, are you?

Evolution is also having a field day when it comes to our daily lives. It makes us impose all kinds of rules on ourselves about how we operate within society.

We just can't get enough of order. We are compelled to get into a queue even if there's only two of us. Odd socks send us into a frenzy of fretting. We put order into our knicker drawers and heaven forbid that our knives and forks could cohabit in the same sections. We get very uncomfortable around those mavericks who dress a bit differently, and we're highly suspicious of Mrs Jones at number 34 who has a different coloured front door to everyone else.

We love order so much that we even impose rules within rules. Take the humble queue, for example. Researchers at University College London found that there are even scientific rules that we humans follow when we queue. It's all about 'the power of six'. People will wait for six minutes in a queue before giving up, and are unlikely to join a line of more than six people. Even spacing is subject to the power of six, with gaps of six inches or less between people potentially sparking anxiety or stress.

Society hates chaos. Schools. Businesses. Governments. They are all terrified of chaos. They think that chaos is the same as anarchy. It isn't. Chaos is what will liberate you from dronedom.

THE ANTIDOTE: Get comfy with chaos

You're going to need to work on having a healthy disregard for and distrust of order. Question whether it's the kind of everyday useful order that is giving you the extra mental capacity to think about something far more interesting, or whether it's the kind of oppressive order that is enfeebling your creative lion. Grrr.

You need to get comfortable in living with disorder. It's going to be tiring. Your brain is going to be over-revving as you force it to work harder than it has ever worked before. So, start slowly. Don't get overwhelmed and give up; get used to disorder a little bit at a time. A small dose of disorder in an otherwise ordered world. It's a big step towards releasing some more of your creative magic.

Everyone would have you believe that chaos is destructive. A menace. Something to fear. It isn't. Run towards it. Play with it. Stroke it. Tickle its ears. Rub its tummy. Chaos is a wonderful, positive force for good. Getting comfy with chaos will open your mind to a far more creative world. And the nudges in this section will hopefully help you to feel more at home with the idea of giving birth to a dancing star.

1.

Stick a fork in it

Let's start with a nice easy nudge. The knife and fork nudge.

Go to your cutlery/flatware drawer. Mix a few spoons in with the forks and sprinkle a couple of knives in with the spoons. How does that feel? A bit uncomfortable? Yes? Marvellous. No? Even more marvellous. We call this chaos priming. It's like stretching before a run.

Now, up the ante a little. Eat with whatever you take out of your newly chaotic cutlery drawer. And don't worry if you make a mess. So much the better. Evolution 0, Creativity 1. Just don't lick your knife whatever you do. That's not the kind of chaos you're after just yet.

2.

Find a new angle of attack

Ever noticed how troubling it is when one of the pictures or mirrors on your wall is wonky? You are now going to inflict the pain of that disorder onto yourself. No need to go mad here though. We're not asking you to make all your pictures and mirrors wonky. That would suggest a pattern, and that's the last thing you want. No. We only want you to put the mirror that you look in every day at an angle. So that every day when you check yourself before you leave the house you are framed by disorder.

3.

Sock hop

The next nudge is equally undemanding but just a little more public. Start by opening your sock drawer. Take all your sock bundles out and put them on the bed. Now unbundle them. Place the individual socks in a pile. Muddle up the pile. Give them a good stir. Now pair them randomly, ideally with your eyes shut to avoid the temptation of trying to find matches.

From now on, you are going to be the odd socks guy/girl. It's a brilliant daily reminder of your commitment to chaos, and one small, sock-wearing step forward in your pursuit of creativity.

Make a chaos corner

You've nibbled at the edges of chaos, now it's time to go all in.

OK, no one is saying you have to live in a mess. It's unhygienic for starters, and we don't want to be responsible for you becoming smelly and antisocial. But if we know that our brains get more creative in a messy environment, then let's create the right environment.

If you're lucky enough to have a spare room, create it there. If you've got a garage or a shed, do it there. But if all you can spare is a corner or a table, that'll work just fine too. It doesn't particularly matter where it is. All that matters is that you have a designated messy space to create or think in – somewhere that you can feel the burden of order and logic lifted. Fill it with whatever you find interesting, the more eclectic the better. And resist theming the things that you put there; clashes are good.

No. Messier than that. Come on. You can do this.

Make a chaos board

Many of us now use laptops as canvases for our creativity, and work in a nomadic combination of WeWorks, cafes, sofas and hot desks. If this sounds like you, you might want to try a more portable version of the messy corner nudge. As we've discussed, our brains will try and impose order on us, and they are often aided and abetted by the algorithms of the websites and apps that we love. Resist their order.

You're going to create 'chaos boards' on Pinterest simply by building boards of everything you like. Colours, designs, photos ... whatever makes you happy or excited. Or angry or sad, come to that. No theme or order – just things you find interesting. Title them 'My Chaos Boards'. Keep the tab open on your browser and continue adding to the boards as often as possible, while ignoring all of Pinterest's well-meaning recommendations. Your brain won't like it, the algorithms won't like it, the order of the universe won't like it, but your creative self will love it.

6.

Pleased to meet you, Your Highness

Right, now we're ready to turn the chaos screw. There's a very good chance that the next nudge will make you feel a bit awkward. In fact, it's possibly closer to a 'shove' than any other nudge in this book. But it WILL make you more creative. Remember that you only need to build one nudge from each chapter into your daily life to make a drastic difference. So, if this one isn't for you, then don't worry about it. Move on.

For one hour of the day, approach every decision as if you were a Disney princess. Would she sing about her feelings? Would she dance along the street? How would she answer the phone? What would she have for lunch? Being you every day brings with it order and certainty. An hour of being your chosen princess will throw everything up in the air, and be a lot of fun. (Chaos can be fun, BTW.) The most important thing is for your brain to enjoy the chaos – this will create positive associations with chaos and free up more of that wonderful creativity that's hiding in there.

If you don't fancy being a Disney princess, how about your favourite character from a book or film? Or the Queen? Or Freddie Mercury from Queen? Just so long as it is someone who is very different from you.

Hopefully, chaos is now starting to feel like the comfiest thing you can think of.

Ghost, Steam, Driver.

Dolls,

Mad,

Tree.

(Answers at the back of the book.)

Don't Settle

How many times have you got a bit over-excited by an idea and spent longer than you spent actually thinking of that idea, thinking of all the reasons why it's so great? Then told it to someone else who responded, 'Hmm. S'OK', leaving you thinking, 'Idiot. It's genius. Obviously just jealous.' Yeah, us too. Don't worry, we all do it.

As a general rule, your first idea is going to be a bit rubbish. Get over it. Truly original and creative answers are not obvious, which means they're rarely the first thing you think of. The most creative thinkers in the world are often the ones who are able to keep looking for longer than anyone else.

Our natural tendencies drive us to choose the first, the obvious and our own when we're looking for answers. We humans convince ourselves that these answers are the right ones because of a host of biological factors. So, it's not your fault. But you need to push past these tendencies. Like Odysseus, you'll have to tie yourself to the mast to resist succumbing to their Siren song. These little nasties will have you believing that you're a genius, a creative demi-god – they'll trick you and seduce you, flatter you and fawn over you. But resist them you must. See them for what they are – the enemies of creativity. You have to fight the urge to convince yourself that OK is great. It isn't. Creative thinking hurts, it demands discipline. If it was easy there'd be a damn sight more of it in the world.

Remember, the first idea is rarely the best one, the obvious idea is never a new one, and our brains are hard-wired to fall in love with our own ideas.

And, if you try to find an answer quickly, you'll find a poor one. You have to be OK with the ambiguity of looking for something different and unfamiliar. But, don't worry, that's what we're here for. A few well-chosen nudges and you'll never fall for any of them again.

The science bit

So, why do we settle for the first idea or an obvious idea? The human mind is incredibly averse to uncertainty and ambiguity, as we mentioned in the previous chapter. From an early age, we respond to uncertainty or lack of clarity by generating plausible explanations. Once we have them, we don't like to let them go, which is why we can often struggle to get past that first idea.

The culprit here is **mental availability**. We are predisposed to be influenced by the ideas or thoughts that are most easily brought to mind. In evolutionary terms we developed this response to enable us to make quick decisions in response to threatening situations.

In 1972, the psychologist Jerome Kagan suggested that resolving uncertainty was one of the main determining factors of our behaviour. When we're faced with heightened ambiguity and unable to immediately gratify our desire to understand or solve, we become highly motivated to find clear-cut answers as quickly as possible and act on them. We want to eliminate the distress of the unknown. We want to achieve '**cognitive closure**'.

Increased need for cognitive closure can bias our choices and influence our preferences. In our rush for definition, we're inclined to come up with fewer hypotheses and search less thoroughly for new information. We become more likely to form judgements based on early cues. This is known as '**impressional primacy**'. As a result, we become more prone to using our first impressions as anchors for our decisions and not properly taking other possibilities into consideration. It's unlikely that we even realize how much we are biasing our own judgements. An example of this that you will almost certainly have experienced is checking into a hotel. Without realizing it, your entire stay will be coloured by this moment. Have a bad check-in experience and you'll spend the rest of your visit unconsciously searching out neutral experiences that will support that opinion: 'Breakfast is a bit bland here' or 'the lifts take absolutely ages' or 'the staff don't talk to me in the corridor'. If you have a good check-in experience, you go around confirming that belief: 'The staff are so friendly when they go about their business.' Check out hotel review sites. Bad reviews regularly start with a poor early experience.

Mental availability drives us to settle with what we know, and confirmation bias assures us that we must be right. Confirmation bias means that we fill in the blanks to suit the answer we've already convinced ourselves is right. And the more we look for THE answer, the more we risk being clouded by what we already know.

Hence the danger of *trying* to find the answer. You will find it, and it will be the wrong one. But you won't know that, because you'll have convinced yourself of its rightness. It takes time and mental energy to get beyond the obvious answer, yet all of our cognitive wiring is demanding that we come up with something reassuring, and pronto.

A man and his son are in a terrible accident and are rushed to hospital in need of critical care. At the hospital, the surgeon looks at the boy and exclaims, 'I can't operate on this boy, he is my son!' How could this be?

The stepfather?

No ...

C'mon ...

It's the mother.

Like it or not, humans are unconsciously biased. Just as we have a blind spot in our field of vision, our unconscious minds contain hidden biases that affect our behaviour. The study of unconscious bias was pioneered by Harvard psychologist Mahzarin R. Banaji. As Banaji makes clear in her 2013 book, *Blindspot*, these biases are survival mechanisms dating back millions of years and hard-wired into us. Humans are continually bombarded by information, but we can process just forty bits a second, so our brains take shortcuts. Rather than stopping to consciously evaluate the appearance of a predator – a process that could take several seconds – our ancestors' unconscious biases screamed danger so they could run away quicker.

These unconscious biases still kick in whenever we see someone not like ourselves. They also reinforce the basest stereotypes. In this instance, the riddle above trips us up because we don't instantly think of women as surgeons.

Society also imposes these patterns and impressions upon us, influencing the availability of potential solutions. The 'mentally salient' or more 'known' pops into our mind, influencing our confirmation. Another reason why we love following fashions and trends – despite the line about it being an expression of your individuality, it's a great example of mental saliency and confirmation bias.

We're also programmed to be rather delighted with our own ideas or efforts. It's called the 'IKEA effect'. (It's why you're so attached to that bookcase that you built.) And when we're pressured to come up with something quickly, these feelings become intensified, making it even harder to kill off your own ideas if you're time pressured. You dig your heels in and love them even more.

Then there's the 'endowment effect', otherwise known as the 'eBay dilemma'. We value things that we own far more than things we don't. So, the price you might be willing to sell *your* laptop for is likely higher than the amount you'd be prepared to pay for someone else's second-hand laptop.

And it's no different when it comes to one of your ideas versus someone else's. Evolution is against us even on this one. We have been designed to trust our own perceptions. Millions of years of evolution have fine-tuned a system to take information from our senses to our brains. The vast majority of this system is automatic and unconscious; scientists estimate 95 per cent of our daily decision-making is automatic. In other words, we take our own ideas to be true and beyond question. We don't even know we are doing it. In fact, pilots have to be rigorously trained to trust their instruments. It's rare that a pilot won't be told to ignore the sensation of which way up he thinks his plane might be, in favour of reading the instrument panel. This is tough and takes training. For millions of years we have been able to trust our sensory input, but it was calibrated for an atmosphere on the ground. When we are travelling at 800 km/h (500 mph) in the air, banking, diving, twisting and turning, the finely tuned systems in our ear canals that tell us which way is up are no longer quite as reliable.

That's a lot of science there to fight against. You're going to need to be vigilant because it's not always easy to know when you have succumbed. Just being aware that you might have is a move in the right direction.

THE ANTIDOTE: Keep going (and going)

Be relentless in your pursuit of original thinking. Through the wind and rain and snow, plough on. Be brutal in your assessment of ideas. Yours and other people's. 'Being nice' about creative ideas benefits no one. (Being a dick isn't helpful either, BTW.) The journey to great thinking is littered with frustration, arguments, upset and self-doubt. A lot of self-doubt.

Creative thinking isn't all flat whites and high fives. It's tough, lonely and slow. There are one or two flat whites and high fives, but generally, it's a bit less blue-sky thinking and a bit more grey-cloud thinking. Anything worth doing is never easy. And when you find that shimmering jewel of inspiring originality, the difficulties of the journey will all be forgotten.

Try to avoid setting yourself an amount of time to come up with an idea. (We'll talk a lot more about the relationship between time and creative thinking in Chapter 8.) Avoid thinking that you've 'cracked it'. Always believe that there is something better. Keep making notes as if all your ideas have the same worth; it will stop you falling in love. Then come back later, or on another day, and review them all when you can see them more objectively.

Push past all those clingy and needy first thoughts. Brush them aside with confidence and stride on purposefully towards a more brilliant creative place.

Remember,
you only need
to choose one.

1.

Thirty boxes

Let's start with a nice easy nudge. Think of this as doing a few creative lunges or star jumps. It's like limbering up before a run or practising scales before you sing. It's all about preparation.

Take a pad of Post-its and count out 30 notes. Set a timer for 15 minutes. Go. Fill every note with whatever's in your head. All crazy thoughts welcome, relevant to what you're hoping to achieve or otherwise. Stick them on the wall as you go. When you've finished, turn your back on all that mentally available nonsense and start the real work. Remember, they're lunges, not ideas. You're in the zone now. Time to kill it for real.

2.

Killing kittens

On the subject of killing things, this next nudge is going to take a bit more discipline.

You're going to commit to killing your first idea for evermore. Every precious, fluffy little darling you ever have. Dead. This is the nudge where you'll need to harden your heart to their wide-eyed appeal or they'll be purring on your lap before you know it. You're not going to throw that idea away, though.

Create a doc on your laptop or buy an exercise book. Title it 'First Thoughts'. In it, write your first thought for whatever it is that you're thinking of. Then don't look back. Not until months/ years later when the doc/book is full. You'll be shocked at just how ugly those little kittens really were. If you still think that one of them is cute, then take it out and play with it. Happy days. Bet you don't though.

3.

Let it go

Yes, we sang this when we wrote it down too. You're going to feel a bit daft doing this, but it's worth it.

Next time you can't get past an idea or thought and it's blocking you from moving on to something more interesting, you are going to channel your inner Elsa and roam through your house, apartment, school, office, library or wherever you go to think and sing the Disney classic at the top of your voice. It's a great way of reminding yourself what you've learned about your need to hang onto first thoughts, ideas and your own little kittens. It will also do a good job of encouraging your brain to look at the problem in a new way. It could be that the bit of the brain you were using wasn't where the answer was – engage another bit and you might find it there instead.

4.

Love it or hate it

It's never easy sharing your ideas for the first time. As long as it's only in your head, it's beautiful and perfect. But at some point it is going to have to withstand contact with the world. The truth is that everyone is better for having someone to bounce ideas off, because you can't know your own blind spots.

The worst thing that can happen when you do finally share it is that someone quite likes it. Thinks it's nice. Doesn't mind it. If that happens, move on. The responses you're looking for are love or hate. Either one works. An extreme reaction one way or another means that you're onto something. Press on.

5.

Chase the churn

You're going to tune into your feelings for this one, so it could take a bit of practice. Emotion is central to our ability to make decisions. That's because the wiring to the brain at this point in our evolutionary history means that connections from the emotional systems are stronger than connections from the cognitive systems.

When your brain comes across something that renders it confused or threatened in some way, you get an unpleasant feeling in your gut well before you have time to get into some kind of rational analysis. This automatically leads you to reject the thought as a way to protect yourself.

Next time it happens, celebrate. You might just have thought of something interesting.

6.

The mañana nudge

It's easy to fall in love with ideas; it's harder to fall out of love with them. But the overnight test is always a good way to discover if your love will last.

Before you go to bed, write down your amazing idea as clearly as possible on a piece of paper and put it on your bedside table.

Then go to sleep.

When you wake up in the morning, before you do anything else, re-read your idea. Your mind will be at its clearest right now, so it will be honest with you. Still excited? No? Don't worry, there are plenty more ideas in the sea.

When it comes to creativity, you should always put off until tomorrow what you could do today.

Hockey, Skate, Vanilla.

Washing, Railway, Dancing.

(Answers at the back of the book.)

Be un- rea- son- able

Oh dear. You can hear that disapproving voice already, can't you? 'You're so unreasonable!' Generally, it's used pejoratively when you don't agree with someone and you doggedly stick to your guns, or you don't want to toe the line in some way. We're not sure that we have ever heard it used as a compliment or term of endearment. But it should be. Unreasonable people should be treasured. Everyone should aspire to be unreasonable. We love unreasonable people because they have a belief in something – a passion, a vision of a better something, the courage to challenge conventions.

George Bernard Shaw clearly thought highly of them. 'The reasonable man adapts himself to the world; the unreasonable one persists in trying to adapt the world to himself. Therefore, all progress depends on the unreasonable man.' History bears this out. The inventors, the artists, the designers, the writers, the scientists, the statesmen, the engineers who have had a hand in pushing humankind forward have all shared this behavioural trait.

Creativity is the pursuit of truth and progress. An unfamiliar idea that confounds the orthodoxy. A new idea that changes everything. It's a gnawing, persistent need to go against the grain. It blinds you to the niceties of polite society ... of reasonable people. Reasonable people don't like to make a fuss. Don't want to disagree or challenge. Don't want things to get awkward. Reasonable people struggle to be truly creative or original, because reasonable people struggle to overcome their need to be liked. Creativity demands that you are prepared to be unreasonable in your pursuit of it, regardless of the consequences. Nothing truly creative and original was ever brought to the world by a reasonable person. The choice is yours.

The science bit

As is so often the case, it all boils down to food and sex. Fortunately, we've come a long way from our ape ancestors. Had we not and you were on a train right now, or in a coffee shop, there would be eyes getting gouged out, rough sex, screeching and a lot of stealing of each other's lattes.

So, what has changed? Why do we now consider elbows on the table rude, and not even consider gouging out the eyes of those sitting next to us? Human nature has developed to fit in and compromise. Social bonds and the need for connection are even more important to us than food. Our friends can always bring us food if we need it, but if we leave our friends for food then we're on our own. So, when it comes to being unreasonable, we've learned that it makes more sense to keep in line.

From an evolutionary perspective, adults who formed attachments would be more likely to reproduce than those who didn't, and long-term relationships would increase the chances that the offspring would reach maturity and reproduce.

So, not only did we evolve to be reasonable, we then codified our reasonable behaviours into social norms. In other words, we have established societies on the basis of acceptable behaviours. And we ostracize those who don't adhere to them.

Since the dawn of civilization, we have been presented with societal conventions that discourage us from being seen as difficult. From Erasmus' 1530 handbook *On Civility in Children*, through etiquette texts from Amy Vanderbilt and Irene Davison, all the way to modern examples like Debrett's, we are obsessed with being seen as agreeable, well mannered and well behaved. A quick online search using the word 'etiquette' will prove just how much of an obsession it is.

During the Enlightenment (broadly, the eighteenth century), a self-conscious imposition of polite norms and behaviours became a symbol of upper-class gentility. The upwardly mobile middle class increasingly tried to identify themselves with the elite through their adopted artistic preferences and their standards of behaviour. They became preoccupied with precise rules of etiquette, such as when to display emotion, how to act courteously, and the art of elegant

dress and graceful conversation. Influential on this new obsession was a series of essays on the nature of politeness in a commercial society, penned by the philanthropist Lord Shaftesbury in the early eighteenth century. Shaftesbury defined politeness as 'the art of pleasing in company'.

'Politeness' may be defined as the dextrous management of our words and actions, whereby we make other people have a better opinion of us and themselves.

Basically, to achieve acceptance in society we tend to do things that we know will get us liked. It can be as simple as paying a compliment or opening a door, or it can be behaviours that are seen to benefit everyone, such as volunteering or sharing. As a species we display a greater level of altruism than any other, so it is clearly something that has benefited us through time. A big part of whether we like others depends upon whether they have traits that we consider likeable. Being unreasonable is not a likeable trait. In fact, it challenges everything that we understand and accept as the basis of our society, so we reject it from an evolutionary standpoint and from a psychological standpoint. We're hard-wired to reject unreasonableness. Well, we did say that this wasn't going to be easy.

We are attracted to people who have personality traits we consider likeable (generosity, kindness) and we are not attracted to people with what we perceive to be undesirable

traits (arrogance, rudeness). This tendency – known as
the **'fundamental principle of liking'** – was validated by
experiments carried out by Elizabeth Tenney, Eric Turkheimer
and Thomas Oltmanns in 2009. These demonstrated that we
are attracted to those whom we consider similar to ourselves,
and we are much more likely to be attracted if those traits are
considered desirable. So, from a species-survival perspective it
does us no good to have negative personality traits.

We also reject the temptation to be unreasonable because it
causes us actual physical pain when we are ostracized. Feeling
left out of the group goes against the fundamental human needs
of belonging and self-esteem. The dorsal anterior cingulate
cortex is a region in the brain that registers physical pain, but it
is also capable of feeling a **'social injury'**.

When you think about it, the brain is doing something
rather clever. The humans who survived were the ones who
worked well in the tribe. So, the brain evolved a system that
translates any 'poor social behaviour' into physical pain. It's like
having your own 'unreasonable taser' to stop you doing things
that will harm your chances of survival.

We have also evolved to focus on the loss of a given scenario
far more than the gain. This is known as **'loss aversion'**.
Unreasonableness really takes a toll here. That's because the
lizard brain, the oldest part of the brain, responsible for your
fight or flight survival instinct, kicks in and is programmed
to mitigate loss. So we go reasonable; a bird in the hand. We
convince ourselves that we're assessing the situation in a
measured, sensible way, but the truth is we haven't yet evolved
to do that – we're being governed by our panicky inner lizards.

There does, however, appear to be one upside to being
unreasonable (other than the betterment of original thinking,
of course). In his 2011 book *The Need to Be Liked*, clinical
psychologist Dr Roger Covin linked this evolutionary trait to
all manner of psychological problems. He listed alcohol and
drug use, being overly career driven, being overly self-critical,
entering into disastrous relationships, staying in disastrous
relationships and excessive focus on self-appearance as just
some of the downsides of our human desire to be liked.

So perhaps being a people pleaser isn't all it's cracked up to be.

THE ANTIDOTE: Agree to disagree

As you have undoubtedly concluded by now, being unreasonable is going to be tough – it takes a brave soul to see it through. It will get everyone around you bristling. It will create a head wind that you'll have to run into. It will lead to friction where there was none before. And it hurts physically. You are going to need to be OK with that. And it will take practice. It's like building up calluses on your hands to toughen them up for manual labour.

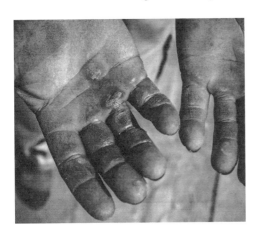

There is hope that you won't be entirely rejected by society, as long as you are being unreasonable for a genuine reason. Being authentic with an unpopular opinion can still be attractive. Being genuine and honest is essential to being likeable; people gravitate towards those who are genuine because they know they can trust them. No one likes a fake. It is difficult to like someone when you don't know who they really are and how they really feel.

So, make sure that you are being unreasonable for genuine reasons. People will then be more inclined to agree to disagree – to acknowledge that you have a difference of opinion and that you are both at liberty to follow your own courses, rather than cast you out into the cold.

But it will still take courage and confidence. You are going to need to create safe spaces and coping mechanisms to deal with the feeling. And that is exactly what the following nudges will help you with. As ever, remember that it is better to choose one nudge and embed it into your life than to play at a number of them. You can always add a second or third in time.

The unreasonable egg timer

Like all pain, the pain you will experience as a result of people's reactions to you for being unreasonable will pass. You'll get over it.

Set a timer for 30 minutes. In those 30 minutes allow yourself to feel bad. Have a good wallow. Feel affronted, misunderstood, hurt, angry. Get it all out. Indulge yourself.

When the buzzer goes, you'll feel much better. Dust yourself off and get on with the business of being unreasonable. Don't dwell. You'll be on the road to something brilliant, and those who made you feel unwelcome or unloved will be on the road to nowhere you'd ever want to go anyway. Wave to them as they disappear into the distance.

Bite your finger not your tongue

Just to be clear here, I'm not advocating that you do yourself any significant damage. But if social pain can manifest as physical pain then you're going to need to create a distraction to avoid it.

Studies carried out in Germany by the researcher Taras Usichenko and others have identified what has become known as the 'cough trick'. In experiments during which groups of men were instructed to cough at the same time as receiving a needle, results indicated that the cough was enough of a distraction to lower the pain of the needle.

Next time you experience a little social pain as a result of your unreasonable behaviour, be brave: bite your finger, not your tongue.

3.

It's OK to burp

You're going to need a safe space for being unreasonable – a place where it's considered perfectly reasonable to be totally unreasonable. No one who harbours a reasonable point of view is allowed to come near it. Could be a sofa, a room or a shed. Whatever works.

Just remember, something is only unreasonable because it feels a bit societally uncomfortable. So, you're going to create new societal norms in your space. You can make them whatever you want. It's your space. Your society. Your norms.

For example, in some societies it is polite to burp. Perhaps burping and farting is the height of good etiquette in your safe-space society. So, buy yourself a fizzy drink/can of soda. Drink it. Burp. Whatever makes you feel comfortable and happy. It's your place to feel good about being unreasonable.

4.

Wear the black hat

The baddie in early cowboy films would always be easy to recognize because he'd be wearing a black hat, while the hero would be in the white Stetson. So, if you want to be unreasonable, if you want to think like the outsider, you need to get into character and dress like one. How good does that feel?

Next time you go off in pursuit of something exciting and original, do so in a black cowboy hat. Make it a reminder that you're pushing out against the orthodox and the ordinary. Then when you've finished being unreasonable and creative, just take it off and hang it up until the next time.

If you don't fancy a black cowboy hat, this trick works just as well with a pair of 'don't mess with me' hi-tops or an 'UP YOURS' T-shirt. Although why you wouldn't want to take the opportunity to wear a black cowboy hat is beyond us.

What would Gaga do?

OK, so you think that you're smashing through the rule book. You're a fresh-thinking, change-making, out-of-control hurricane about to lay waste to the dull minds of suburbia.

Anything is only unreasonable in context. Everything is relative. Just how unreasonable is your idea? Is it actually as unreasonable as something REALLY, REALLY unreasonable?

Wearing a blue dress to a premiere feels pretty anarchic if everyone else is wearing black. But what if you turn up wearing a dress made entirely of meat? Like Lady Gaga did. Imagine your unreasonable idea in the context of that.

Think to yourself on every idea you have, what would Gaga (or your own originality heroine) do? Think about the most extreme, most radical, most 'this would get me fired' version of your idea. Is it a meat dress?

6.

What's the best that can happen?

OK, being unreasonable might feel uncomfortable but have you imagined what could happen if you're right? What if that idea that absolutely everyone hates, and even you aren't sure about, turns out to be a game changer?

You might save lives, save mankind, change the course of history, win a Nobel Prize, have statues erected in your honour, have a film made of your life, become richer than you knew was possible, be revered throughout history, become more quoted than Einstein.

Extreme ideas lead to extreme outcomes. Feel good about being unreasonable. Imagine the best that could happen, not the worst.

Fresh, Donor, Type.

Father,

Dinner,

Home.

(Answers at the back of the book.)

Hate Consensus

It's true to say that hating consensus is a form of being unreasonable. They are both affected by our need to be liked and fit in. But there are distinct differences. Being unreasonable is defying the orthodoxy of the day, if that orthodoxy stands in the way of progress. Hating consensus is focused entirely on opposing the outcomes of group decisions or opinions. It's a belief that good decisions are rarely group decisions.

'A camel is a horse designed by committee', as the great car designer Alec Issigonis once said.

All sorts of strange things happen in groups or herds; all manner of wonky dynamics come into play that are the antithesis of creativity and originality. These dynamics are becoming increasingly common practice in the modern workplace. Consensus leads to an abdication of individual responsibility. Rarely does this result in anything other than the lowest common denominator.

Let us give you an example. Opposite is a diagram showing bullet holes on returning Allied planes that encountered Nazi anti-aircraft fire in World War II. After much discussion among military authorities, all agreed that those areas should be reinforced. A perfectly reasonable decision.

Everyone agreed except for a Hungarian mathematician called Abraham Wald. He pointed out that this was the damage to the planes that made it home. He argued that they should armour all the places that didn't have bullet holes, as that was where all the planes that didn't make it home were obviously hit. He saved countless lives by not accepting the consensus view.

No matter how much they try to convince you that they are right, no matter how sure they are, there must be no swaying you. No matter how many of them believe it, if you don't, say so. Don't give in to group pressure. And if you find yourself agreeing with them, question why.

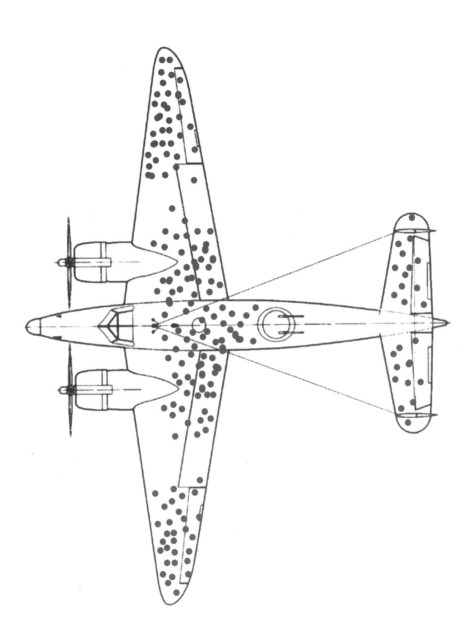

The science bit

As we saw in Chapter 6, we generally prefer people who think like us. It's known as '**consensual validation**'. We're less keen on people who don't. Meeting people who share our ideas makes us feel more confident in our own attitudes about the world. If you love cats, meeting a fellow cat lover shows you that loving cats is OK, and maybe even a virtue.

Groups can lend more certainty to our own opinions. They become echo chambers of confirmation bias. This is known as '**group polarization**'. It means that like-minded people reinforce one another's viewpoints. Group polarization strengthens the opinions of each person in the group.

In a 1969 study by French psychologists Serge Moscovici and Marisa Zavalloni, participants were asked for their individual views on two topical issues: General de Gaulle and Americans. They were then asked to discuss each topic as a group. The researchers noted that individual views – whether favourable or negative – became intensified after they had been discussed with others who held the same view. The results indicated that when we see our opinions reflected by others, our belief in those opinions becomes stronger. That's how consensus works. An over-inflated opinion of the group's rightness, often based on little more than uncertain opinions. Scary, right?

As we've already established in Chapter 6, we humans need other humans. Particularly ones who belong to the same tribe as us. But this tribalism can impair our decision-making.

Psychologists have identified three different types of group conformity, based on the nature and depth of the consensus that occurs. The first, and lowest level of conformity is '**compliance**', which is when our public behaviour changes but our private beliefs stay the same. For example, telling someone you like sport because they do, when deep down, you secretly hate it. The second is '**identification**', when both your public behaviours and private beliefs change, but only in the presence of the group. For example, enjoying drinking with your work friends, but not wanting to drink when you're away from them. The last and most significant level of conformity is '**internalization**'. This is typically a long-term change, when a person alters their public and private behaviours and beliefs, irrespective of the presence of the group. For example, initiating or changing religious or political practices.

You've almost certainly done all of the above. We all have, mostly for the sake of group cohesion. But it can have alarming consequences. Social psychologist Solomon Asch's experiments in the 1950s were some of the first to identify this. In his studies, groups of students were asked to compare the lengths of three different lines (A, B, C) against a fourth. One of these lines was the same length as the fourth, the other two lines being either longer or shorter. Each participant was asked to tell the group which line they thought matched the fourth. Easy. Well, yes, ordinarily, except all but one of the participants were actors. The actors were instructed to agree unanimously on an incorrect response and the real participant was seated in such a way that they always responded last. Without the actors, less than 1 per cent of people got the task wrong. But in the group, Asch found that 37 per cent of participants selected the incorrect line when swayed by the group. This experiment has been replicated many times since and the results are always similar; the group dynamic sways responses. People agree rather than go against the group, even when they know that the group is plainly wrong.

Sometimes we do what other people do in order to avoid professional stupidity and sticking our necks on the line. Defensive decision-making occurs when we are more likely to suggest a sub-optimal but accepted solution rather than an optimal unusual solution. This happens with creativity a lot. As we've discussed, original things make people nervous.

We evolved to want to survive. And those who survived tucked themselves into the pack. Back in the day, if you saw your pack running in fear, you would join them without question, unless you knew something that they didn't. The '**selfish herd theory**' states that lots of animals will clump together not just because others are doing it, but because it minimizes their chance of being eaten. It's deeply ingrained in us from our early ancestors, and you'll use it to navigate the world without even being aware you're doing it. A lot of stock market bubbles have been put down to herd behaviour in the markets.

These 'monkey see monkey do' behaviours are rife in our society. You're 7.1 times more likely to smoke if your friends do. Whether you eat chicken with your fingers or a fork at the dinner table, whether you shave or sport a beard, or how close you think it's OK to stand next to someone on a train platform is all determined by the behaviours of others. We don't always have perfect information to make the best decisions, so we are adept at making the 'best guess' by observing others.

Our brains are always trying to conserve energy. Having to think of everything for ourselves and not benefiting from the experience of others is a waste of energy, so over time, our brains have cleverly developed the skill of learning from others – a sort of pre-programmed energy-saving device. It's one you need to short-circuit.

THE ANTIDOTE: Positive dissent

It's good to question the group. Even better if the group welcomes being questioned. Explain to them the benefits. Tell them that '**positive dissent**' has been employed by many successful organizations throughout history. If they aren't keen, you have to question why.

In 1587, during the reign of Pope Sixtus V, the Catholic Church decided to assign one special dissenter to find and present reasons why nominated candidates should *not* be canonized as saints. This person was referred to as the Promoter of the Faith or, more commonly, the 'devil's advocate'. Taking special care to consider a dissenting view provided an alternative perspective that strengthened their decisions. In 1983, Pope John Paul II reduced the scope of the role, with the result that during his reign almost 500 people were granted sainthood – a great many more than during previous centuries. While it's difficult to compare the quality of decisions before and after the reform, the impact of the policy on the Church's decision-making process is clear.

Another example comes from Alfred P. Sloan, the head of General Motors (GM) from the 1920s. During a meeting in which GM's top management team was considering a weighty decision, Sloan closed the meeting by asking: 'Gentlemen, I take it we are all in complete agreement on the decision here?' Sloan then waited as each member of the assembled committee nodded in agreement. Sloan continued, 'Then, I propose we postpone further discussion of this matter until our next meeting to give ourselves time to develop disagreement and perhaps gain some understanding of what this decision is about.'

What Sloan was looking for was something many of us seek to eliminate: dissent. There's a lot of discussion on how leaders ought to cast a vision, gain buy-in, or steer a group to consensus. There's a lot less discussion on how leaders ought to cultivate a culture that values the right kind of criticism. Criticism and dissent, Sloan recognized, had the power to influence decision-making for the better.

Be proud to be a positive dissenter – only good things will come of it. These nudges will prepare you.

THE NUDGES

Remember,
an only dose
by no means.

Dissent yourself

First rule of dissent club is check your ego at the door. The key word here is 'positive'. The world is full of people who have to win an argument or want to be the player in the room. They aren't dissenting in pursuit of creativity and truth. Make sure you aren't one of them. You might have a different opinion, but you might also be wrong – you might be reacting against someone you don't trust or like much. Remember the messenger effect (page 26)? Dissent discerningly. Dissent sparingly. Dissent with care. Dissent when it matters. But always dissent because you truly believe in what you are saying. And if you don't, don't. Ask yourself: 'Is my dissent positive?'

The dissenter who cries wolf very quickly gets ignored.

Small acts of dissent

Start small. Build up your resilience to dissent by micro-dosing. Find everyday opportunities to go against the grain. Two or three a week is plenty.

Try to avoid being annoying to others, however, as you need to associate dissent with feeling positive. Dress up on dress-down Friday. When you're alone in the lift, stand facing the back. Leave the bathroom door open when no one else is in the house. Do dry February (but don't tell anyone). Only put photos on Twitter and words on Insta. Now make up your own. These are just stretches to warm up your dissenting muscles. Go easy.

Slowly build yourself up to a little positive dissent in public. And if you are going to graffiti, then please use a water-based paint. (Positive dissent, remember?)

The stool of positive dissent

Remind yourself constantly that you are the outlier. You're there to be the lone voice, to call out the group thinking. The dissenter.

A physical reminder of that detachment can be a stool. Only one person can sit on a stool at a time. No one cosies up with other people on a stool. Buy a stool, put it in your office, in your spare room, wherever you think, and when you need to make a decision, sit on it.

It's hard not to get swayed when everyone is going with the flow. So, remove the temptation. Go it alone. Back yourself. We believe in you.

Ask an imaginary friend

Maybe dissenting makes you feel really uncomfortable. After all, as we've mentioned already, it really does go against our default settings. So, why not ask a friend to do it for you? But not just any old friend, an imaginary one. They don't have that default setting. Create your alter ego and when you aren't feeling quite brave enough to dissent, get them to step in.

Think Sasha Fierce, Beyoncé's courageous other self that goes out on stage with her. She's afraid of nothing and no one, let alone being the focus of attention for enormous crowds. Or perhaps your imaginary friend is Louis Theroux. He would never let a question go unsaid, or a dubious dogma go unchallenged, regardless of how intimidating the situation was.

The great thing is, this imaginary friend can be anyone you choose. The moment you can feel a positive dissent coming on, call on them. They'll be only too happy to speak up for you. That's what imaginary friends are for.

Whoa, Neddy

Now, it's easy to imagine that you are always going to be the clear-minded thinker who can see through the confused or malignant consensus. Unfortunately, that won't always be the case. Yes, really – despite all your best intentions. We can all get carried away with the herd when everyone is galloping off in the same direction following a charismatic person or intoxicating thought.

It happens. Agreeing is so much easier and more pleasant than disagreeing. You're only human. So, before you go into that group, or that meeting, or that session, create a little reminder to yourself.

Draw the number 10 on your hand. Whenever you feel yourself getting swept along, count to ten. Pause. Take a moment to decide if this is what you really think is the right thing to do. And if it is, then great. The group is right sometimes. If it isn't, dismount.

6.

Reward yourself

I always think of this as the jelly bean nudge. It's ridiculously simple yet incredibly powerful. And it tastes good too. This is all about **positive reinforcement**. Do the right thing, get a treat – the same behavioural principle that trainers use on dogs. This increases the likelihood of repeating the right behaviours.

Take a handful of your favourite sweets or candy (or a family-sized bag, depending on how sweet your tooth is and how big a reward you think you are likely to need) with you into a meeting or workshop or wherever you think that you are likely to come across group thinking.

Put them where you can see them, then don't touch them. They are off-limits. Only when you have resisted the lure of agreeing with everyone can you treat yourself. Before you know it, you'll be positively dissenting all over the place.

Wise,

Work,

Tower.

Home, Sea, Bed.

(Answers at the back of the book.)

DON'T RUSH IT

Hopefully, by now you're raring to test your newly found abilities to think differently. But before you do, you need to put everything you've learned into the context of this chapter. This may well be the most important chapter of all – for one simple reason.

> **'Productive people move through the tasks they have to accomplish in a systematic way. They make steady and measurable progress toward their goals [...] Creative enterprises rarely involve steady and measurable progress. Instead, being creative involves trying lots of different possibilities, struggling down several blind alleys before finding the right solution.'**
>
> *Time Pressure and Creativity in Organizations: A Longitudinal Field Study.* Harvard Business School Working Paper

This seminal paper in 2002 was the first to prove that time pressure prevents creative thinking. They found that under extreme time pressure, your ability to think creatively drops by an alarming 45 per cent.

Without your realizing it, the world is coercing you into speeding up. It celebrates instant gratification, promotes the prodigious work ethic, cheers on the voracious polymath. And it's messing with your creative mojo. We've allowed it to become the boss. We jump when it demands everything instantly. We live in a world where it has become unacceptable to say, 'It's not ready yet'.

When you consider how everyday life has speeded up in the last two decades, you start to understand that many of these changes have come at a cost to creativity. The instant hit we get from technology, social media and our phones is training us away from all the key principles of creativity. Innovation speeds life up. Embrace it. It's awesome for many things. But remember to carve out the time to be creative. It may feel rather strange at first, even counter-intuitive, but that's the key.

Hold your line and don't be bullied. Creativity demands that you buck the trend. It's not selfish, it's selfless. The world needs creative thinkers, so take your time.

The science bit

No matter where you are in the world, from the USA to the UK, from Ireland to Indonesia, we all work over 1,700 hours in an average year, and we spend one third of our time asleep. That's almost 200 days a year either working or sleeping. And if you then add to that the cleaning, cooking, shopping, washing, bill paying, ironing, queuing, waiting, commuting and all the other things you'd rather not be doing, it's no wonder we all feel that there's never enough time left for doing new or exciting things. Let alone finding the time to sit quietly and explore creative ideas. In fact, one in two Brits believe that 'there aren't enough hours in the day to do everything I'd like to do'. Now, here's the interesting bit. This isn't just a work thing: 61 per cent of students and 44 per cent of unemployed people agreed, too.

So, what's going on? There are a number of explanations. One is that our perception of time is affected by the world around us. The difference between reality and perception has widened since the adoption of information processors, such as phones and computers, which make it feel like time is speeding by and we're under more pressure than ever to keep up.

'We're trying to emulate the technology and be speedier and more efficient. Technology primes us to increase that pacemaker inside of us that measures the passing of time.'

Dr Aoife McLoughlin, Lecturer in Psychology, James Cook University, Singapore

Your environment is another huge factor in your ability to lose yourself down a rabbit hole of creativity. Some of the areas of your brain required for creative problem-solving can only be activated when you let your mind wander. But in the ubiquitous open-plan workspace there's little chance of that. Hands up who still works in an office with its own door and walls? OK, so pretty much no one. Innovative thinking comes from extended concentration, the ability to follow an idea or thought down a network of new paths. And that means being left alone for long periods of time – not being constantly disturbed by people asking you if you're busy because you don't look busy, staring out of the window with your feet up on the desk.

Research carried out in 2005 by Dr Glenn Wilson at London's Institute of Psychiatry found that persistent

interruptions and distractions at work had a profound effect on workers. Those distracted by emails and phone calls saw a 10-point fall in their IQ – twice that found in studies on the impact of smoking marijuana. Your '**default mode network**', active when you daydream, is central to your ability to generate creative ideas. In fact, people with the least mental stimulation – those who are left alone – are 40 per cent better at creative problem-solving. A recent study by the University of California, Irvine, indicated that every time you are interrupted, refocusing your mind can take up to 23 minutes. So actually, you're being ridiculously more productive by staring out of the window with your feet up. Tell them to stick that in their pipes and smoke it.

Another modern working practice that is counter to creativity is the belief in and adherence to multi-tasking. It's a scientific fact that the human brain is actually incapable of multi-tasking.

> 'When you try to multi-task, you typically don't get far enough down any road to stumble upon something original because you're constantly switching and backtracking.'
>
> Earl Miller, Professor of Neuroscience at MIT

1.

Turn downtime into boomtime

You may know that because of your internal body clock, your energy and alertness levels experience peaks and troughs throughout the day. But did you know that you are most optimized for creative thinking during the parts of the day when you're lowest in energy? At these points, your brain is less vigilant and you have fewer inhibitions, making it easier for abstract ideas to form.

So, make the most of them. Before breakfast. After lunch. Before bed. Whenever they are. Make those your designated creative-thinking times. Set calendar reminders to block them out and make them official. Put your phone in another room. Remove yourself from distractions and start daydreaming. Obviously, the more time you can give yourself the better, but this will be a start.

2.

Become a single tasker

You won't find a simpler nudge in this book. But don't let its simplicity fool you – it's also one of the most powerful. It is a fail-safe way to give yourself the headspace you need to generate ideas. It's as simple as the name suggests. Do one thing at a time. When you've done it, do the next thing.

The pen is mightier than the keyboard

You are significantly better at understanding and processing information when you write things down by hand. This is because the slowness of writing by hand demands heavier 'mental lifting', forcing you to engage more deeply and focus on what's important. So, you're less open to being disturbed, and more likely to stay in the creative moment for longer.

When you're staring at your screen and nothing is flowing, try putting pen to paper instead.

Ban the S-word

We all know that time pressure can lead to feelings of panic or anxiety. But did you know that one of the best ways of combating time-induced anxiety is to reframe it as excitement? It's a bit like that thing you learned in physics: the first law of thermodynamics. Energy is never lost; it can only be transformed from one form to another.

Ban the S-word. Try 'active' or 'in demand' instead.

Hey Alex, how are you? Active, man. Super active.

5.

Get a room

If you're at work, build walls. Block yourself in. Put up screens. And if you can't, sit in a cupboard. An empty meeting room. In the basement bike park. Shut yourself in anywhere you won't be disturbed. It really doesn't matter what anyone thinks. When the quality of your creative thinking goes through the roof, they'll all just think you're a mad genius. If you're at home, shut yourself away in the quietest spot you have. And make sure you put your phone and laptop in a different room.

6.

Give up

Yes. Give up. Go and do something else. The harder you try to squeeze it out, the less likely it is to come. Let the other parts of your brain have a go. Go for a walk. Have a dance. A bath. Bake a cake. See what happens.

Tooth, Potato, Heart.

Washing,
Sex,
Learning.

(Answers at the back of the book.)

Failure Is an Option

'IF YOU PLAYED GOLF AND YOU HIT A HOLE IN ONE ON EVERY HOLE, NOBODY WOULD PLAY GOLF, IT'S NO FUN. YOU'VE GOT TO HIT A FEW IN THE ROUGH AND THEN GET OUT OF THE ROUGH, THAT MAKES IT INTERESTING.'

Warren Buffett

Failure is an essential component of success in creative and original thinking, and it happens far more than success. See it as a positive, rather than something to feel ashamed of – shame and guilt are the two biggest barriers to embracing failure.

Looking for original answers will take you into uncharted territory. Google won't be there to bail you out. You'll be on your own. Failure is inevitable; repeated failure highly likely. Be pleased. Every failure is another marker on the map of where not to go, helping you to understand better where to look for success. Every failure must spur you on and give you confidence. Because success only comes to those who never stop looking for it.

Countless memes, posters, coffee cups and so on tell you to embrace failure. It seems that everyone understands that it's a good thing. But no one ever tells you why we find it so difficult to do, or how to achieve it. We're going to change that.

The science bit

According to a 2018 report from the Global Entrepreneurship Monitor, roughly one third of 'wantrepreneurs' allow a fear of failure to prevent them from starting a business.

The fear of failure is very common. But there are two distinct groups of failure fearers – the Over Strivers and the Self Protectors – and failure fearers are split almost equally between the two. Which one are you? The **Over Striver** avoids failure by succeeding. Fear of failure underpins much of what the Over Striver does, and therefore many of the factors that are associated with fear of failure – anxiety, low self-esteem, perception of a lack of control – are still felt.

The **Self Protector** avoids the personal implications of failure. They will do everything in their power to mitigate the extent to which failure reflects poorly on their abilities and self-worth. Self Protectors may employ either defensive pessimism, by setting unrealistically low expectations prior to events in which they may be evaluated, or self-handicapping, so that failure is seen as related to an impediment and not because of low ability.

This is the only chapter that doesn't have its roots in evolution. So, where does our fear of failure come from? Well, it's entirely a product of society, rooted in parental socialization and parent–child relations. But before you start getting too worked up about how much your parents have messed you up, chances are they had no idea that they were doing anything other than loving you. They most likely had a fear of failure baked into them by their parents, and so on and so on.

A parent's fear of failure is known to be an indicator of a child's fear of failure.

Mothers who have an increased fear of failure are more likely to withdraw love from their child when their child makes a mistake or fails, and this love withdrawal leads to fear of failure in the child.

School then does a great job of reinforcing these negatives. Remember putting your hand up to answer a question? Remember what happened if you got it wrong? Of course you do. Getting the 'right' answer the first time was all that was rewarded. Wrong answers are punished in a variety of ways throughout your school career: low grades, scolding, contempt, even humiliation from teachers and peers. Not exactly an environment to explore the positive upsides of failure. It's a very rare school that embraces a reward system for innovative behaviour.

These learned behaviours compound in young minds the belief that failure is totally unacceptable and carries with it negative implications for self-worth and relational security. Hardly surprising then that we seek to avoid failure at all costs.

Anyone with a high fear of failure is more inclined to see the *possibility* of failure. This in turn exerts pressure on them to succeed beyond their capacity. And sooner or later, when the occasional failure occurs, as it always does, no matter how hard we try to avoid it, the response is all the more damaging to our well-being.

Shame is another driver of failure avoidance, particularly among those who are less sure of their abilities and as such are more likely to have low self-esteem. They tend to be more dependent on, susceptible to, and influenced by external approbation. Interestingly, people with either high or low self-esteem may feel equally down about a failure. However, the same pattern is not exhibited with respect to feelings of shame and humiliation. Those with high self-esteem do not exhibit the same feelings.

Perfectionists are chronic sufferers of '**failure fear**'. Perfectionism is determined as an excessive concern over making mistakes and the need to avoid them. Because those mistakes are perceived by the perfectionist as failure.

A failure of one's own high personal standards. A failure to live up to 'their perception of' high parental expectations. A failure to avoid 'their perception of' high parental criticism. A failure in the quality of one's actions. And a failure to adhere to one's own preference for order and organization.

That's a lot of failure. And a lot of fear.

The upside of perfectionism is that it drives high standards of performance, which is why it can be interpreted as a positive trait, but sadly it always comes at a cost. This high performance is always accompanied by the severe criticism of one's own behaviour. Performance must be perfect, or it is worthless. Any minor flaw constitutes failure. This is more of an issue in those with low self-esteem, who feel intense shame after a setback. Perfectionism in someone with low self-esteem is known to be a cause of psychological problems, including anorexia, depression and obsessive-compulsive disorder (OCD). To feel love and approval, they must perform at ever-increasing levels of perfection – which is, of course, unsustainable.

THE ANTIDOTE: Fail happy

You're really going to have to put yourself out there to embrace failure; whether you are an Over Striver or a Self Protector, whether you have high or low self-esteem. We need you to start to see failure in a different way – a way that makes you feel good about yourself. Because the pursuit of original and creative outcomes is going to be littered with failure. They demand risk.

You are going to reframe failures as learnings. Because if you don't fail then you never learn anything. Bill Gates once said that 'success is a lousy teacher', and we're not sure that anyone would consider him a failure.

Start to think about everything that you've learned from a particular failure. What has it taught you? How will it help you to move forward stronger than before? See every setback as an opportunity to discover something new. And start to look forward to learning new things.

Every failure is a lesson. Learn to learn that, and soon you'll be loving your failures and feeling pretty good about yourself.

THE NUDGES

Remember,
you only need
to choose one.

1.

You're in good company

The trouble when most of us fail at something is that we don't admit to it unless we really have to. We bury it away and it festers. So, when people do fess up it is incredibly inspiring and reassuring. And sometimes that support is all we need to carry on.

Surround yourself with those of the quotes over the page that strike the strongest chord with you. Print one on a T-shirt or a coffee cup. Tattoo one on your arm. Frame some. Whatever it takes to keep them in your eyeline. Then whenever the need arises, they'll be there for you. Use them to remind yourself that your failure was only a step towards your success.

'IT IS IMPOSSIBLE TO LIVE WITHOUT FAILING AT SOMETHING, UNLESS YOU LIVE SO CAUTIOUSLY THAT YOU MIGHT AS WELL NOT HAVE LIVED AT ALL. IN WHICH CASE, YOU FAIL BY DEFAULT.'

J.K. Rowling

'I HAVE NOT FAILED. I'VE JUST FOUND 10,000 WAYS THAT WON'T WORK.'

Thomas Edison

'Failure is a greater teacher than success.'

Clarissa Pinkola Estés

'Failure is unimportant. It takes courage to make a fool of yourself.'

Charlie Chaplin

'Success *is* 99 per cent failure.'
Soichiro Honda

'A queen is not afraid to fail. Failure is another stepping-stone to greatness.'
Oprah Winfrey

A champion is defined not by their wins but by how they can recover when they fall.
Serena Williams

If you are making mistakes,
then you are making new things,
trying new things, learning,
living, pushing yourself,
changing the world.

Neil Gaiman

The exorcism nudge

Don't worry, it's not as scary as it sounds. And hopefully won't leave you traumatized for the rest of your life.

We all share a tendency to exaggerate the scale of our failures. They are way scarier and burn far brighter in our eyes than in anyone else's. One way to keep them under control is to write them down. Call them out for what they are. Write out what it is that you are scared of, and how you think that you are going to fail. You'll be amazed at how much less scary they will seem.

Now for the real exorcism. Get a candle and a box of matches. Burn those bits of paper. Burn them all – watch them turn to ashes! Feel better now? Course you do.

Turn failure into a hobby

Hobbies are fun, harmless ways in which we occupy our time. We look forward to doing them. What if failing was your hobby? For failure to be an option you have to get comfortable with it. Let it into your life in a way that is less troubling to you. Take it off the big scary pedestal that you've placed it on.

Take up a hobby that you will fail at. It's the failure that makes the hobby fun. Bake a soufflé – no one can do that! It'll be rubbish (but probably very tasty), and fun to make. Rent a trumpet for the day. Take a life-drawing class. Kayak. Whatever. You'll be hopeless at them all. Brilliant. But you'll spend more time laughing than crying. Failing can be fun when you're failing at things that don't matter. You'll then start to associate that fun with failing and begin building some positive failure muscle memory. And just imagine what you'll learn in the process.

No experience is ever wasted.

Up your failure rate

To succeed you have to fail a lot. If you don't, you aren't trying hard enough. Seriously. The most successful people ever are also the biggest failures.

J.K. Rowling's original pitch for the Harry Potter series was rejected 12 times before she was offered a publishing contract. The books have now sold over 400 million copies and been translated into over 65 languages. Rowling is now the highest-paid author in the world, according to *Forbes* magazine.

A.P. McCoy was the British National Hunt Champion Jockey for an unprecedented 20 years in a row, meaning that he rode more winners every year for 20 years than any other jockey. He also rode more losing horses every year for 20 years than any other jockey, simply because he rode more horses than any other jockey. That is the mentality of a winner who has accepted failure as a necessary step to success, and is undeterred by it.

Don't avoid failure, it's inevitable. Embrace it. Set your failure target high.

The more you fail, the sooner you'll win.

Frame your failure

This is a nudge in two parts.

First, literally frame it. Find yourself a funny frame. Put the fail in the frame. It will take the sting out of it. How bad can it be framed in pink fake fur? Unless of course it is an absolutely earth-shatteringly bad fail. Then the frame might not be entirely successful. Which leads us neatly on to the second part of this nudge.

This is about putting the failure in context. Is it really as bad as you first thought? Create a one to five scale. Was it really a five? Keep checking back with the furry frame. There's a very good chance that it will keep sliding down in time.

Just fucking do it

This is the last nudge of the last chapter. We've saved our favourite nudge (and the use of a swear word for emphasis) for this very moment. OK, so there comes a point in life, and in this book, when all the planning, all the preparing, and all the talking can't take you any further. No one can help you if you aren't prepared to do it for yourself.

Imagine that you are standing on the top diving board at your local pool. Your toes are gripping the edge of the board, you peek over at the water, your heart is pounding like crazy. You either allow yourself to roll forward right now, or you never will.

Or as Joe Cabot said in *Reservoir Dogs*, 'You know how to handle that situation? Shit your pants, and dive in and swim'.

Creativity demands that you do exactly that. You'll be so glad you did.

Bell, Clock, Fire.

(Answers on the next page.)

RAT ANSWERS

CHAPTER 1
Sausage, Chilli, Hot. DOG.

Cabbage, Work, Eye. PATCH.

CHAPTER 2
Socket, Lid, Brow. EYE.

Crystal, Foot, Snow. BALL.

CHAPTER 3
Copy, Tom, Bob. CAT.

Tight, Works, Mark. WATER.

CHAPTER 4
Ghost, Steam, Driver. TRAIN.

Dolls, Mad, Tree. HOUSE.

CHAPTER 5
Hockey, Skate, Vanilla. ICE.

Washing, Railway, Dancing. LINE.

CHAPTER 6
Fresh, Donor, Type. BLOOD.

Father, Dinner, Home. TIME.

CHAPTER 7
Wise, Work, Tower. CLOCK.

Home, Sea, Bed. SICK.

CHAPTER 8
Tooth, Potato, Heart. SWEET.

Washing, Sex, Learning. MACHINE.

CHAPTER 9
Cry, Front, Ship. BATTLE.

Bell, Clock, Fire. ALARM.

REFERENCES

CHAPTER 1
Car accidents happen near the home
'One in Three of All Car Accidents Happen a Mile From Home', *Daily Telegraph*, August 2009.

Inattentional blindness
Arien Mack and Irvin Rock, *Inattentional Blindness*. Cambridge, Massachusetts: The MIT Press, 1998.

Arien Mack and Irvin Rock, 'Inattentional Blindness', *Psyche*, 5(3), 1999.

Daniel J. Simons and Christopher F. Chabris, 'Gorillas in Our Midst: Sustained Inattentional Blindness for Dynamic Events', Perception, vol. 28, 1999.

Habituation
K. Cherry, 'What is Habituation', About.com, 27 December 2013.

P.M. Groves and R.F. Thompson, 'Habituation: A Dual-Process Theory', *Psychological Review*, 77(5), 419–50, 1970.

C.H. Rankin et al., 'Habituation Revisited: An Updated and Revised Description of the Behavioral Characteristics of Habituation', *Neurobiology of Learning and Memory*, 92(2), 135–38, 2009.

R. Thompson, 'Habituation', in *International Encyclopedia of the Social & Behavioral Sciences*, 6458–62. Oxford, UK: Pergamon, 2001.

Non-dominant hand = more creative
Lucia Capacchione, *The Power of Your Other Hand: Unlock Creativity and Inner Wisdom Through the Right Side of Your Brain*. Pompton Plains, New Jersey: Career Press, 2001.

CHAPTER 2
Great Wall of China
'China's Wall Less Great in View from Space', nasa.gov, 9 May 2005.

Sleepwalking
Giuseppe Plazzi, 'Sleepwalking and Other Ambulatory Behaviours During Sleep', *Neurological Sciences*, 26, 193–98, December 2005.

Lying 100 times a day
Pamela Meyer, *Liespotting: Proven Techniques to Detect Deception*. New York: St. Martin's Griffin, 2010.

Messenger effect
Robert M. Arkin (ed.), *Most Underappreciated: 50 Prominent Social Psychologists Describe Their Most Unloved Work*. New York: Oxford University Press, 2011.

S.M. Kassin, 'Deposition Testimony and the Surrogate Witness: Evidence for a "Messenger Effect" in Persuasion', *Personality and Social Psychology Bulletin*, 9(2), 281–88, June 1983.

Milgram obedience test
Stanley Milgram, 'Behavioral Study of Obedience', *Journal of Abnormal and Social Psychology*, 67(4), 371–78, 1963.

Obedience/cues of authority
Joop van der Pligt and Michael Vliek, *The Psychology of Influence: Theory, Research and Practice*. New York: Routledge, 2017.

Concreteness effect
F. Jessen et al., 'The Concreteness Effect: Evidence for Dual Coding and Context Availability', *Brain and Language*, 74(1), 103–12, August 2000.

A. Paivio, M. Walsh and T. Bons, 'Concreteness Effects on Memory: When and Why?', *Journal of Experimental Psychology: Learning, Memory, and Cognition*, 20(5), 1196–1204, 1994.

Mere-exposure effect
R.F. Bornstein and P.R. D'Agostino, 'Stimulus Recognition and the Mere Exposure Effect', *Journal of Personality and Social Psychology*, 63(4), 545–52, 1992.

R.B. Zajonc, 'Mere Exposure: A Gateway to the Subliminal', *Current Directions in Psychological Science*, 10(6), 224–28, December 2001.

Confirmation bias
Raymond S. Nickerson, 'Confirmation Bias: A Ubiquitous Phenomenon in Many Guises', *Review of General Psychology*, 2(2), 175–220, June 1998.

M.E. Oswald and S. Grosjean, 'Confirmation Bias', in R.F. Pohl (ed.), *Cognitive Illusions: A Handbook on Fallacies and Biases in Thinking, Judgement and Memory*. Hove and NY: Psychology Press, 79–96, 2004.

Keats effect
M.S. McGlone and J. Tofighbakhsh, 'Birds of a Feather Flock Conjointly (?): Rhyme as Reason in Aphorisms', *Psychological Science*, 11(5), 424–28, September 2000.

M.S. McGlone and J. Tofighbakhsh, 'The Keats Heuristic: Rhyme as Reason in Aphorism Interpretation', *Poetics*, 26(4), 235–44, May 1999.

CHAPTER 3

Sir Ken Robinson
TED talk (June 2006): 'Do Schools Kill Creativity?'

Six basic emotions
Paul Ekman, *Emotions Revealed: Recognizing Faces and Feelings*. London: Weidenfeld and Nicolson, 2003.

Paul Ekman, 'Expression and the Nature of Emotion', in K. Scherer and P. Ekman (eds)., *Approaches to Emotion*. Hillsdale, New Jersey: Lawrence Erlbaum, 1984.

Evolutionary usefulness of sweat
Randolph M. Nesse and Elizabeth A. Young, 'Evolutionary Origins and Functions of the Stress Response', University of Michigan Department of Psychiatry, December 2000.

Neophobia
David T. Corey, 'The Determinants of Exploration and Neophobia', *Neuroscience & Biobehavioral Reviews*, 2(4), 235–53, Winter 1978.

R. Misslin and M. Cigrang, 'Does Neophobia Necessarily Imply Fear or Anxiety?', *Behavioural Processes*, 12(1), 45–50, January 1986.

Good scary
Margee Kerr, *Scream: Chilling Adventures in the Science of Fear*. New York: PublicAffairs, 2015.

Margee Kerr, Greg J. Siegle and Jahala Orsini, 'Voluntary arousing negative experiences (VANE): Why we like to be scared', *Emotion*, 19(4), 682–98, June 2019.

Fast music and risk taking
J.J. Chandler and E. Pronin, 'Fast Thought Speed Induces Risk Taking', *Psychological Science*, 23(4), 370–74, April 2012.

Takemi Fujikawa, Yohei Kobayashi and Foo Yung Chau, 'Effect of Background Music Tempo on Decision Making Under Risk and Intertemporal Choice', Otemon Gakuin University, Osaka / Tokyo Institute of Technology / Universiti Sains Malaysia, 2010.

Arachnophobia
Graham C.L. Davey, 'Characteristics of Individuals with Fear of Spiders', *Anxiety, Stress and Coping* 4(4), 299–314, June 1991.

75% of the people sampled were either mildly or severely afraid of spiders.

Exposure response prevention therapy
'What is Exposure Response Prevention (ERP)?', ocduk.org article.

CHAPTER 4

Apophenia
S. Fyfe, C. Williams, O.J. Mason and G.J. Pickup, 'Apophenia, Theory of Mind and Schizotypy: Perceiving Meaning and Intentionality in Randomness', *Cortex*, 44(10), 1316–25, November–December 2008.

Hito Steyerl, 'A Sea of Data: Apophenia and Pattern (Mis-) Recognition', *e-flux*, 72, April 2016.

Pareidolia
Masaharu Kato and Ryoko Mugitani, 'Pareidolia in Infants', *PLoS ONE*, 10(2), 1–9, February 2015.

J. Liu et al., 'Seeing Jesus in Toast: Neural and Behavioral Correlates of Face Pareidolia', *Cortex*, 53, 60–77, April 2014.

Messy desk research
Kathleen Vohs (PhD), Carlson School of Management, University of Minnesota, in *Psychological Science*, September 2013.

Queuing research
Professor Adrian Furnham, Professor of Psychology, UCL Psychology & Language Sciences, February 2017.

CHAPTER 5

Uncertainty
Jerome Kagan, 'Motives and Development', *Journal of Personality and Social Psychology*, 22(1), 51–66, 1972.

Mental availability (availability heuristics)
V.S. Folkes, 'The Availability Heuristic and Perceived Risk', *Journal of Consumer Research*, 15(1), 13–23, June 1988.

Amos Tversky and Daniel Kahneman, 'Availability: A Heuristic for Judging Frequency and Probability', *Cognitive Psychology*, 5(2), 207–32, 1973.

Cognitive closure

X. Liu, Z. Zhang and J. Liang, 'Need for Cognitive Closure, Framing Effect and Decision Preference', *Acta Psychologica Sinica*, 39(4), 611–18, January 2007.

D.M. Webster and A.W. Kruglanski, 'Individual Differences in Need for Cognitive Closure', *Journal of Personality and Social Psychology*, 67(6), 1049–62, December 1994.

IKEA effect

Daniel Mochon, Michael Norton and Dan Ariely, 'Bolstering and Restoring Feelings of Competence via the IKEA Effect', *International Journal of Research in Marketing*, 29(4), 363–69, December 2012.

Michael Norton, Daniel Mochon and Dan Ariely, 'The IKEA Effect: When Labor Leads to Love', *Journal of Consumer Psychology*, 22(3), 453–60, July 2012.

Endowment effect

Keith M. Marzilli Ericson and Andreas Fuster, 'The Endowment Effect', *Annual Review of Economics*, 6(1), 555–79, 2014.

Carey K. Morewedge and Colleen E. Giblin, 'Explanations of the Endowment Effect: An Integrative Review', *Trends in Cognitive Sciences*, 19(6), 339–48, June 2015.

95 per cent of decision-making is automatic

Daniel Kahneman, *Thinking, Fast and Slow*. London: Penguin, 2011.

CHAPTER 6

Forming attachments is good for evolution

R.F. Baumeister and M.R. Leary, 'The Need to Belong: Desire for Interpersonal Attachments as a Fundamental Human Emotion', *Psychological Bulletin*, 117(3), 497–529, June 1995.

Etiquette and politeness

Desiderius Erasmus, *On Civility in Children*, 1530.

The Amy Vanderbilt Complete Book of Etiquette, 1952.

Irene Davison, *Etiquette for Women*, 1928.

Fundamental principle of liking

Elizabeth R. Tenney, Eric Turkheimer and Thomas F. Oltmanns, 'Being Liked is More than Having a Good Personality: The Role of Matching', *Journal of Research in Personality*, 43(4), 579–85, August 2009.

Social pain as physical pain

Giovanni Novembre, Marco Zanon and Giorgia Silani, 'Empathy for Social Exclusion Involves the Sensory-Discriminative Component of Pain', *Social Cognitive and Affective Neuroscience*, 10(2), 153–64, February 2015.

Loss aversion

Daniel Kahneman, Jack L. Knetsch and Richard H. Thaler, 'Anomalies: The Endowment Effect, Loss Aversion, and Status Quo Bias', *Journal of Economic Perspectives*, 5(1), 193–206, Winter 1991.

Richard H. Thaler, Amos Tversky, Daniel Kahneman and Alan Schwartz, 'The Effect of Myopia and Loss Aversion on Risk Taking: An Experimental Test', *The Quarterly Journal of Economics*, 112(2), 647–61, May 1997.

The need to be liked

Roger Covin, *The Need to Be Liked*, 2011.

The cough trick

Dr Taras Usichenko, various publications, including 'Reducing venipuncture pain by a cough trick: a randomized crossover volunteer study', *Anesthesia & Analgesia*, 98(2), 343–45, September 2004.

CHAPTER 7

Plane survivorship bias

Abraham Wald, 'A Method of Estimating Plane Vulnerability Based on Damage of Survivors'. Statistical Research Group at Columbia University for the National Defense Research Committee, 1943.

Consensual validation (bandwagon effect)

Richard. L. Henshel and William Johnston, 'The Emergence of Bandwagon Effects: A Theory', *The Sociological Quarterly*, 28(4), 493–511, Winter 1987.

Rüdiger Schmitt-Beck, 'Bandwagon Effect', *The International Encyclopedia of Political Communication*, 1–5, July 2015.

Group polarization

Serge Moscovici and Marisa Zavalloni, 'The Group as a Polarizer of Attitudes', *Journal of Personality and Social Psychology*, 12(2), 125–35, June 1969.

David G. Myers and Helmut Lamm, 'The Group Polarization Phenomenon', *Psychological Bulletin*, 83(4), 602–27, 1976.

Cass R. Sunstein, 'The Law of Group Polarization', *Journal of Political Philosophy*, 10(2), 175–95, November 2002.

Asch experiment

Solomon E. Asch, 'Opinions and Social Pressure', *Scientific American*, 193(5), 31–33, November 1955.

Selfish herd theory

W.D. Hamilton, 'Geometry for the Selfish Herd', *Journal of Theoretical Biology*, 31(2), 295–311, May 1971.

Jens Krause, 'The Effect of "Schreckstoff" on the Shoaling Behaviour of the Minnow: A Test of Hamilton's Selfish Herd Theory', *Animal Behaviour*, 45(5), 1019–24, 1993.

7.1 x more likely to smoke

Antti J. Saari, Jukka Kentala and Kari J. Mattila, 'The Smoking Habit of a Close Friend or Family Member – How Deep Is the Impact? A Cross-sectional Study', Department of General Practice, University of Tampere, Tampere, Finland, 2014.

CHAPTER 8

Under time pressure, ability to think creatively drops 45 per cent

Teresa M. Amabile et al., 'Time Pressure and Creativity in Organizations: A Longitudinal Field Study', Harvard Business School Working Paper, April 2002.

Workers work over 1,700 hours a year on average

Source: Organization for Economic Co-operation and Development, 2019.

One in two Brits think there are not enough hours in the day

Source: Target Group Index, 2017.

'What's the time? Examining whether technological advances are affecting our temporal judgements.' (2011) https://dspace.mic.ul.ie/handle/10395/1515

https://www.sciencealert.com/research-suggests-that-technology-is-speeding-up-our-perception-of-time

IQ fall from interruptions at work

'Infomania worse that Marijuana', BBC News, 22 April 2005
Study by Dr Glenn Wilson, Institute of Psychiatry, University of London, 2005

Solitude leads to a 40 per cent improvement in problem-solving

J. Smallwood and J. Schooler, 'The Science of Mind Wandering: Empirically Navigating the Stream of Consciousness', *Annual Review of Psychology*, 66(1), September 2014.

Optimized creativity during downtime

Mareike B. Wieth and Rose T. Zacks, 'Time of Day Effects on Problem Solving: When the Non-optimal is Optimal', *Thinking and Reasoning*, 17(4), 387–401, 2011.

Pen is mightier than the keyboard

Ephrat Livni, 'Keyboards Are Overrated. Cursive is Back and It's Making Us Smarter', *Quartz*, 25 July 2017.

Saperstein Associates, White Paper from 'Handwriting in the 21st Century?' educational summit, 2012.

CHAPTER 9

Fear of failure

Niels Bosma and Donna Kelley, Global Entrepreneurship Monitor, 2018/2019 Global Report.

Ted Thompson and Dale L. Dinnel, 'Construction and Initial Validation of the Self-Worth Protection Scale', *British Journal of Educational Psychology*, 73(1), 89–107, March 2003.

Picture credits

5 Christian J Kober/Alamy Stock Photo; **6a** chinaface/iStock; **6b** Lukas Bischoff/iStock; **16** John Michael Vosloo/Shutterstock; **18** Justine Raybon/Unsplash; **20** Syda Productions/Shutterstock; **27a & b** Kali9/iStock; **29** Granger/Shutterstock; **38** Steve Prezant/Getty Images; **39** Kanade, T., Cohn, J.F., & Tian, Y. (2000). Comprehensive database for facial expression analysis. Proceedings of the Fourth IEEE International Conference on Automatic Face and Gesture Recognition (FG'00), Grenoble, France, 46–53 © Jeffrey Cohn. Used with permission; **40** Yin + Yang, made on behalf of the charity Peace One Day, 2012, by Jake and Dinos Chapman © Jake and Dinos Chapman. All Rights Reserved, DACS 2021; **51** Blue Gum Pictures/Alamy Stock Photo; **52** Panoramic Images/Alamy Stock Photo; **55** Nick Page/Unsplash; **64** Nomad/iStock; **68** Mark Rogers/Alamy Stock Photo; **70** Take Photo/Shutterstock; **77** Barney Burstein/Corbis/VCG via Getty Images; **79** Romano23/iStock; **81** Jerry Tavin/Paramount Pictures/Everett Collection/Alamy Stock Photo; **82** Jon Kopaloff/FilmMagic/Getty Images; **87a** Abramova Kseniya/iStock; **87b** Bouncy/Alamy Stock Photo; **89** McGeddon/CC BY-SA (https://creativecommons.org/licenses/by-sa/4.0); **92** Chad Ehlers/Photoshot/Avalon; **95** 7000/iStock; **103** Keri Wiginton/Chicago Tribune/Tribune News Service via Getty Images; **106** Caron Watson/Shutterstock; **111** Lemon_tm/iStock; **119** beanimages/Shutterstock; **121** Ikonoklast Fotografie/Shutterstock.

Published by
Laurence King Publishing
361–373 City Road
London EC1V 1LR
United Kingdom
Tel: +44 20 7841 6900
Email: enquiries@laurenceking.com
www.laurenceking.com

A catalogue record for this book is
available from the British Library.

ISBN: 978-1-78627-900-2

Picture Research: Giulia Hetherington
Design: Alexandre Coco

Printed in China

Laurence King Publishing is
committed to ethical and sustainable
production. We are proud participants
in the Book Chain Project®.
bookchainproject.com

Acknowledgements

Nichola Raihani,
Head of Experimental Psychology, University College London.

Valeria Trabattoni,
MSc Cognitive & Decision Science, University College London.

Eleanor Heather,
Associate Director at The Behavioural Architects.

Sam Tatam,
Organizational Psychology Consultant.

Dan Bennett,
Behavioural Science Consultant.

Niamh Mahoney,
Research Assistant.